bags
in
bloom

bags in bloom

create 20 unique flower
purses with simple
embroidery stitches and
easy-to-sew patterns

susan cariello

Watson-Guptill Publications

NEW YORK

Contents

Copyright © 2010 by Breslich & Foss Ltd
Text copyright © 2010 Susan Cariello

Photography Sussie Bell
Design Lisa Tai
Illustrations Kate Simunek
Managing Editor Kate Haxell

Conceived and produced by
Breslich & Foss Ltd
Unit 2A Union Court
20–22 Union Road
London SW4 6JP

Library of Congress Catalog Card Number
2009943182

ISBN 978-0-8230-0079-1

Printed and bound in China

10 9 8 7 6 5 4 3 2 1

First American Edition

Introduction

I have been a textile designer for over fifteen years and am incredibly fascinated by old embroidery techniques. I have studied vintage embroidered textiles and antique swatches very closely, using them as inspiration for fresh and exciting new floral designs. Whether you are a dedicated embroiderer, or perhaps someone who has never sewn before but adores handbags, this is the perfect book to inspire you and get you started. From the following pages you will learn how to create your very own stunning, truly original handmade bags that will be the envy of all your friends.

The twenty individual floral bag projects can all be created using the twelve simple embroidery stitches clearly illustrated at the

start of the book. Also illustrated are the assembly techniques that show you how to turn the embroidered fabric into a gorgeous yet practical accessory…a bag.

Each project guides you step-by-step through an embroidered design. You will learn how—by using different yarns, flosses, and wools—eye-catching designs can be created to dramatic effect. Beads, sequins, and vintage and new buttons are used creatively to add detail and sparkle.

You can either follow the projects precisely or use them as starting points, adapting the designs as you wish. By doing this you will be able to create a simply endless range of bags, each of which will be as unique and as individual as you are. I hope that you will enjoy embroidering and making up the bags as much as I do and that you use and love the bags you create.

Susan Cariello

Getting started

Before you begin work on a bag, you should assemble all the materials and equipment you'll need for the whole project. There is little in life that is more frustrating than starting a new project and having to stop halfway through because you are missing a vital ingredient. Fortunately, you don't need anything very unusual to make any of the bags in this book, so read this chapter through and do all your shopping before you start sewing.

Finding inspiration

Before I begin any new project or design, I am fired up by a real sense of passion and excitement. The very thought of creating something fresh and original is a thrill, and my imagination runs away with all the possibilities. From which gorgeous fabrics to use, to which new rayon yarns or chunky wools I could try, combined with which particular embroidery stitches: I revel in the anticipation of how it will all look when the bag is completed.

If you are creating your own bag designs, then finding inspiration is essential to motivate and drive you. Your individual and truly original bags should stand out from the crowd and become your very own.

Creating a mood board

Different things inspire different people and there is no hard and fast rule as to where you should look for ideas. A great starting point is to create a mood board. Buy a pinboard, and plenty of push-pins, from a stationery shop. Mount the board somewhere where you can easily see it: inspiration lurking behind a door isn't much use!

Flip through magazines and periodicals and cut out any images that catch your eye. It could be a particular color sample you like, the latest fashion trend, an interior scene from a designer loft apartment, or maybe just a simple decorative detail from a vintage vase or antique coffee pot.

You could include any postcards that you have picked up on your travels, or remnants of fabrics, or any odd buttons or beads you have stashed away. Bits of yarn, trimmings, found objects that appeal— though you're not sure why—all of these can be sources of inspiration.

By arranging all of these items on your mood board you will begin to see exactly what you like; what colors you are drawn to, and which shapes and motifs often attract you. This is a great way to find inspiration.

▶ *A mood board in my studio. I have several boards and change the contents to help keep my ideas fresh.*

Fabrics and trims

I absolutely love visiting my local fabric shops, wool and yarn stores, and notions counters. I can easily spend hours looking around, collecting swatches of cloth that I like and samples of any ribbons, buttons, and trim that I simply cannot resist. I add these swatches and samples to my mood boards (Why stop at one board?) and they help fuel the creative flames.

Great fabrics and trimmings can also be found in your local vintage stores or antique markets. You want your bag to be as individual as possible, and adding that single, decorative, antique button you found at the bottom of a box at the back of that vintage shop you discovered last month, will make a unique statement.

Flowers and plants

Another tremendous source of endless inspiration comes from looking at flowers and plants. You could simply sketch shapes and ideas from a bunch of flowers that you have bought at the market, or take a field trip to the countryside and collect a few wild

◀ *I bought these big reels of lace from a garment factory that was closing down and I hope that they'll last for years.*

▼ *I love all kinds of flowers and foliage, but particularly those with graphic outlines and clean, fresh colors.*

◄ *Reproduction volumes of antique botanical and zoological illustrations are packed with gorgeous images.*

▲ *This flower (see First Bloom, page 44) was directly inspired by the illustration on the left.*

flowers or fallen autumnal leaves, or simply sit in your garden and absorb what surrounds you.

It's a great idea to keep a small notebook or drawing pad and sketch anything that you like, from how the stems, tiny leaves, and delicate petals of a daisy are formed, to the larger flower heads of classic roses. Don't worry, you don't need to be able to draw these flowers and leaves beautifully. The sketches are for your benefit alone and as long as they contain the information you need, they are absolutely perfect.

Nature is so beautifully formed that whichever flowers and plants take your fancy, they will be a fantastic starting point for your future designs.

Botanical illustrations

Another way to study flowers and plants is by looking at reference books. I have built up a significant library of books that I have collected over the years, and I refer to them whenever I am looking for a slice of inspiration.

My favorite is a treasured volume by Pierre-Joseph Redouté, whose beautiful flower and plant illustrations offer endless possibilities and inspiration for embroidery and appliqué alike. Looking at textile design books for floral patterns and motifs is also an excellent way to get started.

Museums and art galleries

A different way to get stimulated and inspired is to visit museums and galleries. I personally take great pleasure in spending time in textile and costume departments of national and local museums alike, examining the sumptuous fabrics and lavish, antique embroideries on the garments and accessories that are on display.

I get really excited and motivated and take notes of the techniques and stitches used to create the pieces. When I get back to my studio I marry these notes with fabric, yarn, and floss samples, and the results inspire new ideas that will all ultimately feature in my finished designs.

Collecting materials

You have made your mood board, or collected together images, drawings, trimmings, and swatches that have inspired you. You have an idea of which colors you would like to make your new bag in. The next stage is to source the fabrics, yarns, flosses, and notions you're going to need.

Fabrics

The cloth you choose can have a dramatic effect on how your design and bag will eventually look and feel. I absolutely love visiting my local fabric and notions retailers, touching and feeling the different textures before I settle on exactly which cloth will form the basis of my bag. Whether you decide to go to your local fabric store or home decorating fabrics outlet, a market, or a vintage fabric store, there are a few things that you will need to be aware of when choosing fabrics.

Whatever you intend to use your bag for, you will definitely want it to be practical and durable. Fine or lightweight fabrics—such as dupioni silk or fine,

open-weave wool fabrics—look great, but they can prove to be slightly difficult to work with and are not very robust for a daily-use bag. Save these for special-occasion purses.

A good-quality fabric of medium weight and thickness—maybe a tactile, rich, velvety wool or a medium-weight, textured linen—will be a perfect cloth to choose for your first few projects.

Home décor fabrics are also wonderful, as they are heavier and ideal for constructing slightly larger bags. However, be careful not to choose a fabric that is too thick, or your sewing machine may struggle to sew through all the layers when you come to sew up the seams of your bag.

◀ *This patterned fabric was the inspiration for a bag (see Sparkling Leaves, page 122).*

▲ *No bag needs a lot of fabric, so buy just a yard of fabrics that you love and you're sure to use them in a project one day.*

▶ *I have a huge collection of embroidery flosses, which I keep in drawers organized by color.*

For the most part, I prefer to use natural fibers—cottons, linens, and wools—as I find them more malleable and easier to work with, and I love the feel and look they give to a bag.

I have listed exactly which fabrics I have used with each project, but please feel free to use whatever alternative fabrics you like. As long as the fabric you choose is practical, then the choice of color, texture, and pattern is entirely down to your personal taste.

For the lining fabrics I have generally used a plain-colored cotton for the Spring/Summer bags, and a thicker polyester satin fabric for the Fall/Winter ones.

As you make more bags (and I hope you will), and collect different fabric swatches and short lengths, you might find it helpful to color coordinate these into separate boxes. This makes it much easier to find fabrics for future projects. I never throw anything away, as even the smallest swatch could be used in a new bag.

Yarns, flosses, and wools

Collecting together all the yarns, flosses, and wools you will need for your embroidered designs is the next thing to do. As with the fabrics, I have listed which yarns I have used for each project.

As you do more embroidery, you will gain experience of how different threads look and feel and this will give you more ideas for how to use them in future projects. Generally, I have used fine embroidery flosses in shiny rayon and twisted cotton for the more delicate motifs. To create a defined, graphic look in other projects, I have used medium-weight, wool tapestry and knitting yarns.

There are no rules as to exactly which yarns you should choose. For instance, fantastic effects can be

◀ *I store my tapestry and knitting yarns in small boxes, again organized by color.*

▶ *I've collected buttons of all shapes and sizes. I hunt for different sizes and colors at craft fairs, in vintage shops, and online.*

created using the chunkiest of mohair and chenille wools, or even by embroidering with strips of metallic silk organza. Just be aware that if your fabric has an open weave, like a textured wool, you will find it easy to use a thicker yarn to embroider with. If the fabric has a tight, close weave, like dupioni silk, then you will need to use finer threads.

Embellishments

You will need some notions and trims. These can include beads in various sizes and shapes—such as pearl drops, bugle and seed beads—and both cupped and flat sequins, individual ones and those bought in lengths.

You will need a magnetic clasp for each bag. You may also need ribbons, tapes, and buttons in varying sizes and colors, including vintage and new ones.

Interfacing and interlining

Interfacing will be needed to stiffen and strengthen sections of your bag. It comes in varying weights, and can be purchased as an iron-on or sew-in: I use the latter as I find it gives better results.

A heavyweight, woven interlining will be needed to reinforce each bag you make. This can be bought in any good fabric store and adds body, as well as strength, to your creations.
I have used a heavyweight buckram to create the sturdy base where required for some of the bags.

Threads

Sewing threads in matching colors to the fabrics used will be needed to sew up your bag. These can be purchased from your local fabric store.

Beads should be sewn on with strong sewing thread or specialist beading thread, though this comes in only a narrow range of colors.

◀ I have many spools of sewing threads, including decorative threads for machine embroidery.

Equipment

To embroider beautiful flower designs and to make them into gorgeous, individual bags, you will need a few pieces of equipment. You should be able to find all of these in your local notions or fabric store. It might be helpful to invest in a dressmaker's box with individual sections where you can keep all your equipment and threads in order, ready to start your next project.

Basic equipment

1 Embroidery hoops You will need embroidery hoops in various sizes. Don't worry if your design does not entirely fit into the frame, you will just need to carefully move the fabric as you embroider.

Lay the fabric to be embroidered over the inner hoop and place the outer hoop on top. Carefully push the outer hoop down over the fabric and inner hoop. Tighten the outer hoop with the screw at the side. If the fabric is not completely taut, very carefully pull it evenly all the way around the hoop.

2 Needles You will need embroidery needles in varying sizes, depending on which yarns and flosses you will be using. A darning needle will be required when embroidering with strips of fabric. A selection of sewing needles will also be essential, including fine beading needles for delicate embellishment.

3 Pins Long dressmaker's pins with a colored head for easy visibility are best. A pincushion to keep them at hand is easier than a box.

4 Scissors A pair of good-quality fabric scissors will be vital. Have a separate pair for cutting out paper patterns. Small embroidery scissors will be indispensable for precision cutting. A seam ripper is useful for neatly unpicking seams if need be.

5 Markers An HB pencil, a fabric marker, and a white dressmaker's pencil will be needed.

6 Measuring You will find both imperial and metric measurements in this book, so choose your preferred system and stick to it. A ruler and tape measure will be needed, and a set square or pattern square is very useful.

Other basic equipment

Sewing machine A good, solid, sewing machine will be necessary. Mine is over thirty years old and is still going strong, though you will find a lightweight, modern machine will do the job just as well.

Iron A good steam iron to carefully iron out any wrinkles in your embroidery before making up a bag.

Miscellaneous You may also find a metal thimble and a needle threader useful.

◄ *You only need a sewing machine with basic functions to make any of the bags in this book.*

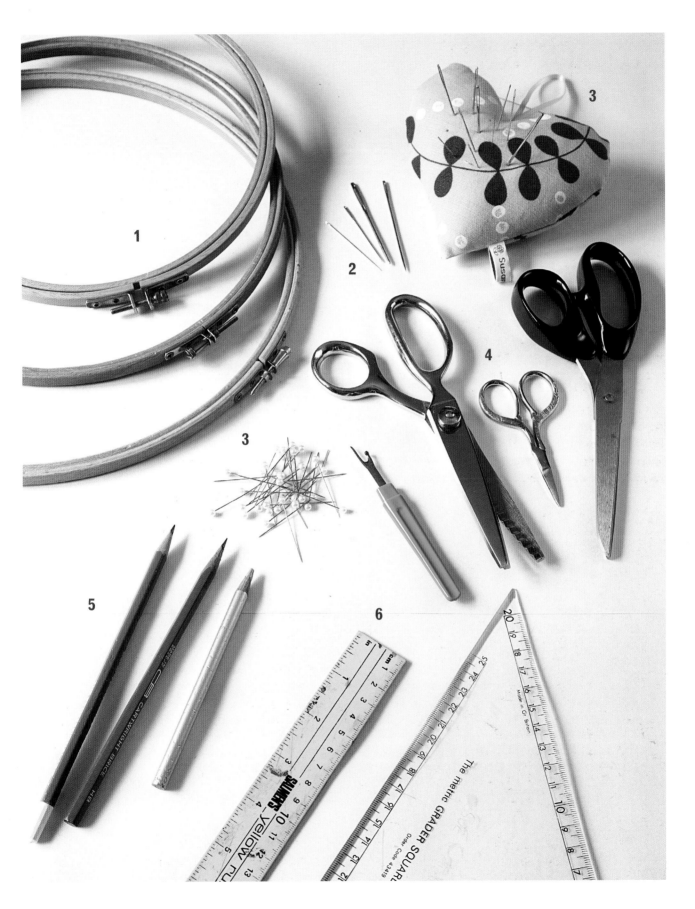

Techniques

I have designed bags for this book using just twelve embroidery stitches, so even if you are a novice sewer, you will find it easy to master the embroidery skills needed. To make up the bags, all you really need to be able to do is sew lines using the sewing machine. The final line of topstitching around the top edge of a bag does need to be straight, so if you haven't done this before, do practice on a scrap of spare fabric before sewing your project.

Stitch gallery

Although just a limited number of embroidery stitches are used to make up the floral designs in this book, working them in different yarns and flosses can give them very different looks.

If you have never done hand embroidery before, start by practicing all the stitches using stranded embroidery floss on medium-weight cotton fabric.

Follow the illustrations carefully and do not pull the stitches too tight or the fabric will pucker.

Once you have mastered forming a stitch, make a little test sample using the project fabric and threads before you start a bag. Different threads and flosses may need to be tensioned differently to make the stitch look good.

Running stitch

The simplest embroidery stitch, this can be used to create flower stems, or to outline flower or leaf shapes.

Following the drawn stitch line, pass the needle in and out of the fabric, making sure the stitches are of equal length. (This can vary according to the look that you want.)

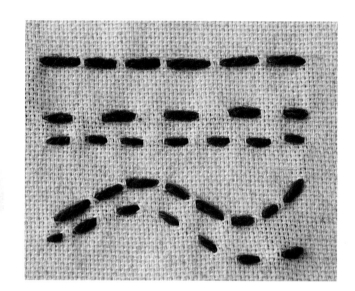

Backstitch

This simple stitch is ideal for stitching a slim flower stem, an outline flower shape, or a leaf design.

Bring the thread through the fabric and make a small, straight, backward stitch. Bring the needle through again a stitch-length in front of the first stitch. Make another backward stitch,  inserting the needle at the end of the last stitch. Continue in this way to form a line of stitches.

Fishbone stitch

This decorative stitch is one of my favorites. It is perfect for creating leaf shapes and looks effective in both thick wools and fine threads.

1 Bring the needle through the fabric at A and insert it at B, forming a small straight stitch.

2 Bring the needle out again at C.

3 Insert the needle at D. Make an upward-sloping stitch and bring the needle through at E.

4 Insert the needle at F, making a downward-sloping stitch that overlaps the previous stitch. Bring the needle through at G.

5 Insert the needle at H, making sure the stitch lies close to the previous one.

6 Continue working the sloping stitches, alternating from side to side, until the shape is completely filled.

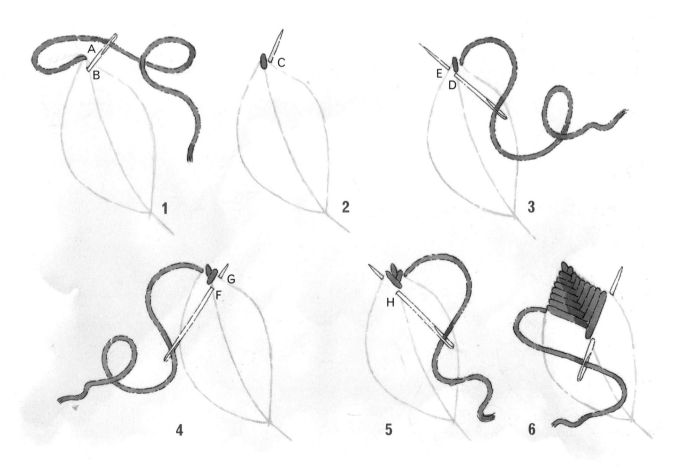

Chain stitch

This stitch can be used to create a thick stem, to outline larger flowers or leaves, or it can be worked in close rows to fill in a shape.

1 Bring the needle through at A. Holding the thread down with your thumb, insert the needle back into the fabric very close to where it came out.

2 Bring the needle out at B, within the loop of thread.

3 Pull gently on the thread so that the loop tightens, then insert the needle back into the fabric at B.

4 Bring the needle out at C, within the last loop of thread.

5 Tighten the loop and insert the needle again at C. Continue in this way until the chain of stitches is the required length.

6 To secure the last loop in the chain, bring the needle up through the fabric within the loop, then make a short straight stitch over the end of the loop to hold it in place.

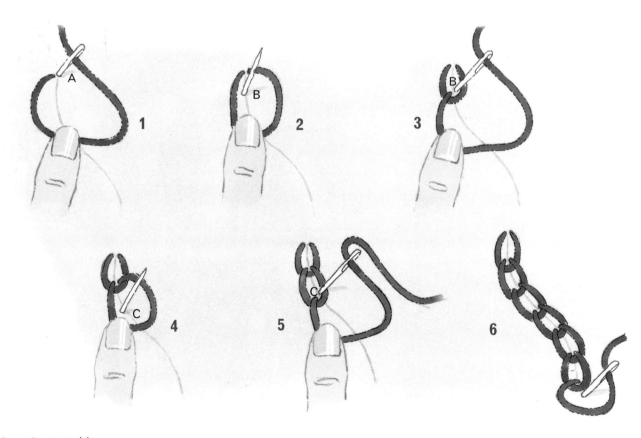

Detached chain stitch

This stitch is worked in a similar way to Chain Stitch (see opposite), but as individual loops rather than a chain. Use a single loop to create a delicate leaf, or work grouped loops to form sprigs.

Bring the needle through at A. Holding the thread down with your thumb, insert the needle back into the fabric close to where it came out. Bring it up through the fabric at B, within the loop. Make a short straight stitch over the end of the loop to hold it in place.

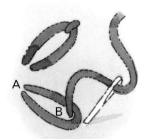

Buttonhole stitch

Also known as Blanket Stitch, this is a very versatile stitch that can be used to form edgings and borders, and even Buttonhole Wheels when worked in a circle.

1 Bring the needle out through the fabric at A. Insert it at B and bring it out again at C, ensuring that the needle passes over the loop of thread.

2 Gently pull the loop taut, then insert the needle at D and bring it out again at E. Continue in this way, securing the last loop with a small, straight stitch.

3 To work a wheel, draw concentric circles to define the inner and outer stitching lines. Work buttonhole stitch in the usual way, but placing the stitches close together on the inner circle and spacing them out on the outer circle.

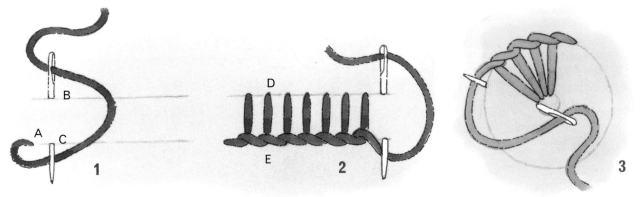

French knot

This delicate stitch can be used singly to form flower centers, or in groups to form tiny flower heads and buds.

1 Bring the needle up through the fabric. Wrap the thread twice around the needle and hold it in place with your left thumb (the thumb isn't illustrated as it would cover the thread).

2 Holding the thread firmly, insert the needle close to where it came out. Pull the thread taut to form a single knot. Alternatively, bring the needle back up through the fabric, as here, at the position of the next knot.

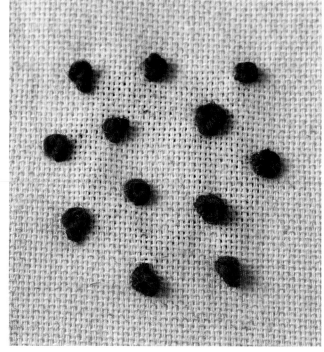

Rose stitch

This stitch creates slightly three-dimensional flowers, especially when worked with doubled yarn.

1 Work a French knot (see above) for the flower center, being careful not to pull the thread too tight. Bring the needle out at A. Insert it at B and bring it out again at C.

2 Taking the thread over the straight stitch just formed, insert the needle at D and bring it out at E.

3 Continue making straight stitches in this way, working around the knot until you have encircled it several times. To keep the flower looking three-dimensional, make sure you don't pull the threads too tight.

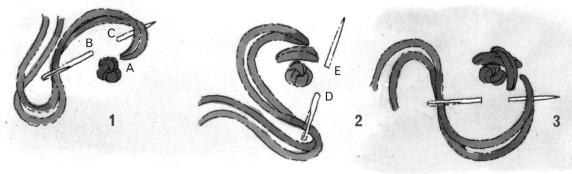

Daisy stitch

A variation on Detached Chain Stitch (see page 23), this stitch can be used to embroider small flowers with about five petals, as above left. The stitches can also be elongated and compressed, as above right, to create larger, daisy-type flowers.

1 The individual loops are worked in the same way as Detached Chain Stitch. Position the starting point of each stitch next to the previous one to form a circle that will be the center of the flower.

2 Make the short, straight stitch over the end of the loop to hold it in place, then bring the needle out through the fabric where you want the next petal to "grow" from.

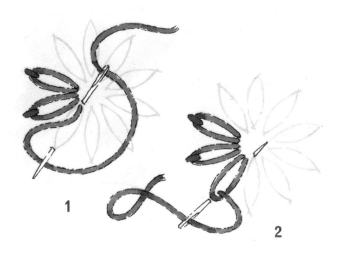

Spider's web stitch

Use this stitch to create circular flowers that can be almost three-dimensional, especially when thick yarns or even strips of fabric are used to do the weaving. Start by drawing a circle to establish the flower shape.

1 Bring the needle up through the fabric at A and insert it at B to make a straight stitch.

2 Bring the needle back up at A, insert it at C and bring it out again at D.

3 Insert the needle again at A and continue around the circle, creating seven evenly spaced straight stitches that form the "spokes" of the web.

4 Thread a darning needle with the yarn or fabric you are going to weave with. Bring the needle up through the fabric at A. Take the needle alternately over and under the "spokes," working around and around until the web is filled in.

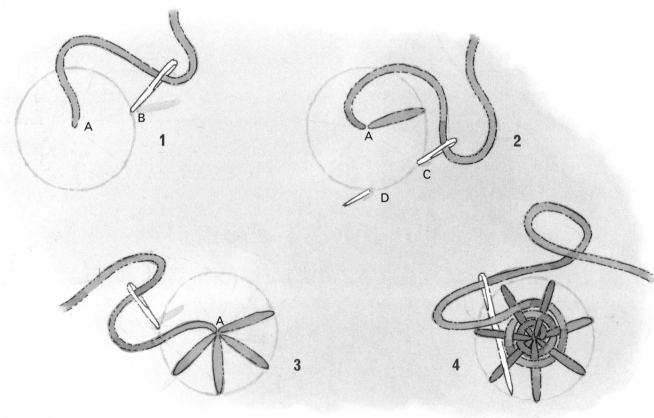

Satin stitch

This simple stitch is perfect for filling in solid areas of a design and is great for creating flower petals. Keep the stitches close together and the edges even to create the smooth look.

1 After drawing out the flower shape, bring the needle through at A and insert it at B.

2 Bring the needle back through at C, right next to A, and insert it at D, right next to B.

3 Continue in this way until the flower has been filled in.

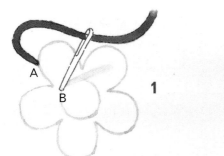

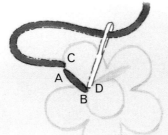

1

2

3

Straight stitch

A simple variation of Satin Stitch (see above), this stitch can be used to create an almost instant flower. Start by drawing a circle to establish the outer edge of the flower.

1 Bring the needle up through the fabric at A and insert it at B to make a straight stitch.

2 Bring the needle back up at C and insert it at B again.

3 Continue in this way all around the circle, spacing the stitches evenly.

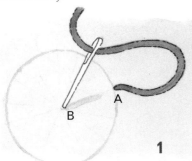

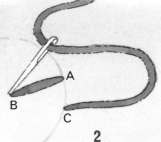

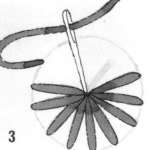

1

2

3

Assembling the bags

There are three main styles of bag—flat bag, bag with a base, and clutch bag. Within these styles there are three variations of a flat bag and two variations of a bag with a base. Each project tells you exactly which assembly instructions to follow to complete the bag shown.

None of the bag styles are difficult to make as they mainly involve nothing more complicated than plain sewing on a sewing machine. Read through the steps before starting a project. If you are at all unsure about anything, then you can always make a test sample using scrap fabric.

Assembling a flat bag

There are three variations on this style of bag. Two variations have darts at the bottom corners to give the bag shape, while the third variation has pleats at the top.

1: Small bag with contrast top, darts, and folded handles
2: Medium bag with darts and lined handles
3: Medium bag with pleated top

1: Small bag with contrast top, darts, and folded handles

These little bags make smart accessories for weddings, lunches, and all kinds of parties. They'll hold all you need for the occasion, and look gorgeous at the same time.

Projects using these instructions
• Bow and bouquet (see pages 52–57)
• Black and cream (see pages 118–121)

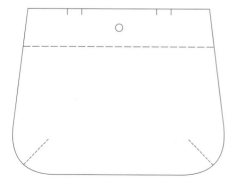

Template 1 (see page 135)

Bag exterior

1 Enlarge Template 1 by 149 percent and cut out the whole shape to make a paper pattern. Pin the template to the interlining and cut out two identical pieces. Set these aside.

2 Cut the bag template along the horizontal dashed line: we'll refer to the small top section as A and the larger bottom section as B. Pin template B to the embroidered fabric. There will already be an outline drawn before you started the embroidery, so match this carefully to the template. Add ⅜ in. (1cm) all around for seam allowances and cut out the shape using fabric scissors **(fig 1)**. Cut out the back of the bag using the same template and plain fabric.

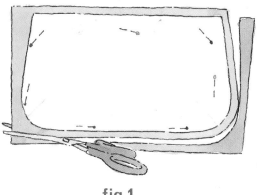

fig 1

3 Pin template A to the contrast top fabric and cut out the shape twice, again adding ⅜ in. (1cm) all around for seam allowances.

4 With right sides together, pin the contrast fabric to the top edge of the embroidered fabric. Set the sewing machine to a medium straight stitch and sew the seam, taking a ⅜ in. (1cm) seam allowance **(fig 2)**.

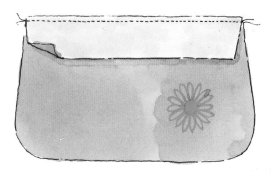

fig 2

5 Press the seam allowances toward the contrast top section. Top-stitch the facing in a matching thread, sewing close to the seam and catching the seam allowances in the stitching **(fig 3)**. Join the remaining fabric pieces (A and B) in the same way to assemble the back section of the bag.

6 Right side out, pin the bag front to one of the pieces of interlining cut in step 1: from this stage on, treat these two layers as one piece.

7 To make the darts, with right sides together fold the top left corner over so that the left-hand side aligns with the bottom edge, and pin the fold in place. From the bottom left corner, measure up 2 in. (5cm) along the fold and mark this point with a pencil **(fig 4)**. Repeat the process on the other edge of the bag front and on both edges of the back of the bag. The dart positions are also marked on the template with dotted lines.

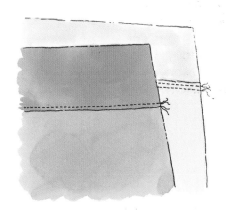

fig 3

8 Sew the darts on the sewing machine. Starting at the outer edge and ⅝ in. (1.5cm) from the fold, sew a straight line to the marked pencil point. Knot the threads to secure the stitching. Sew each dart in this way.

fig 4

9 With right sides facing, pin the bag front and back together, matching the sides, the bottom, and the darts **(fig 5)**. Using the sewing machine, sew around the sides, leaving the top edge open. Turn the bag right side out.

10 Referring to the template, lightly mark the handle positions on the front top edge of the bag with a pencil. Do the same on the back of the bag.

Folded handles

1 Pin the fabric handle pieces to the appropriate pieces of interfacing: from this stage on, treat these two layers as one piece.

2 Along the long sides of each strip, press ⅜ in. (1cm) toward the middle. Then fold the strip in half (so the raw edges are concealed) and press again **(fig 6)**.

3 Set the sewing machine to a medium straight stitch. Using a matching thread, topstitch close to the long open edge of each handle.

4 Trim each end of both handles, making sure they are the same length.

5 Pin the ends of one handle to the right side of the bag front, matching them with the markings from the template. Make sure the handle seam is facing toward the bag side seams on both sides and that the handle is not twisted **(fig 7)**. Pin the other handle to the back of the bag in the same way.

6 Sew each end of each handle in place, stitching ⅜ in. (1cm) from the raw edge. Sew backward and forward over each end a few times to make sure each handle is firmly secured **(fig 8)**.

Bag lining

1 Pin template A to the facing fabric and cut out the shape twice, adding ⅜ in. (1cm) all around for seam allowances. Using the same template, cut out two pieces of interfacing, again adding ⅜ in. (1cm) all around. Right side out, pin the facing pieces to the interfacing pieces and from this stage on treat these two layers as one piece.

2 Pin template B to the lining fabric and cut out the shape twice, again adding ⅜ in. (1cm) all around for seam allowances.

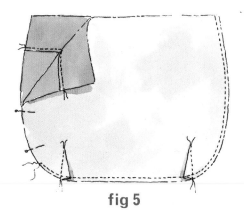

fig 5

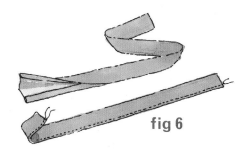

fig 6

fig 7

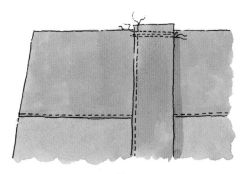

fig 8

3 With right sides together, pin the bottom edge of one facing to the top edge of one lining. Set the sewing machine to a medium straight stitch and sew the pieces together. Press and topstitch the seam as for step 5 of Bag Exterior. Repeat the process with the other facing and lining pieces.

4 With right sides facing, repeat steps 7–8 of Bag Exterior to make a dart in each bottom corner of both the front and back lining pieces.

5 With right sides facing, pin the front and back lining sections together, matching the sides, bottom, and the darts. Using the sewing machine, sew around the sides, leaving the top edge open. Leave the lining with the right side facing in.

6 Referring to the template, mark the position of the magnetic clasp on the right side of one facing. Using a craft knife, carefully cut two small slits, just large enough to insert the prongs of the clasp **(fig 9)**. Insert the prongs into the slits then, following the manufacturer's instructions, slip the retaining disc over the prongs and ensure it is flush against the fabric. Bend the prongs over to hold that side of the clasp in place.

7 Snap the free side of the clasp onto the side attached to a facing. Press the exposed prongs against the opposite facing and mark their position **(fig 9)**. Separate the clasp and attach the free side to the opposite facing at the marked points, in the same way as before. This process will make sure the clasp is aligned accurately on both sides.

Finishing

1 With right sides facing, put the embroidered bag exterior inside the bag lining, matching the side seams and top raw edges. Make sure the handles are pushed down between the two layers. Pin the bag exterior and bag lining together around the top edge.

2 Set the sewing machine to a medium straight stitch. Taking a ⅜ in. (1cm) seam allowance, sew around the top edge leaving an opening between the handles at the back of the bag **(fig 10)**.

3 Turn the whole bag right side out through the gap in the top edge, pulling out the handles and then pushing the lining down inside the bag. Turn in the seam allowances across the gap between the handles.

4 Using a sewing machine and matching thread, topstitch around the top edge of the bag, sewing across the gap to close it **(fig 11)**.

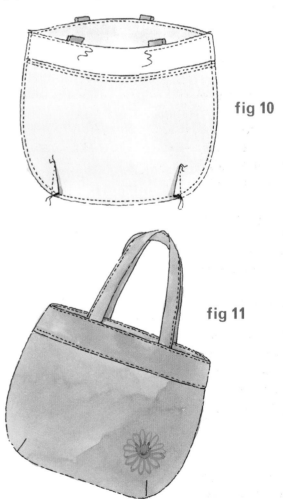

fig 10

fig 11

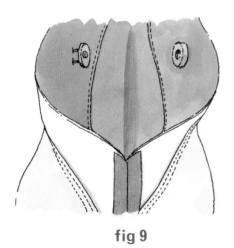

fig 9

2: Medium bag with darts and lined handles

This style of bag is perfect for daily use. Whether you're spending the day in the office or out shopping, it's roomy enough to carry all your necessities without being oversized or clumsy.

Projects using these instructions

- Pink and pretty (see pages 58–61)
- Wildflower days (see pages 76–79)
- Garden fresh (see pages 80–85)
- Summer chic (see pages 86–89)
- Vintage buds (see pages 96–99)
- Fireside glow (see pages 114–117)
- Twinkling lights (see pages 126–129)
- Winter garden (see pages 130–133)

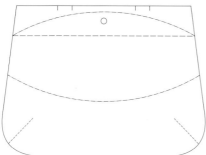

Template 2 (see page 136)

Bag exterior

1 Follow the steps for Bag Exterior in Small Bag with Contrast Top, Darts, and Folded Handles (see pages 29–30), enlarging Template 2 by 161 percent.

Note that if the bag you are making does not have a contrast top, the template does not need to be cut for the Bag Exterior and steps 3–5 can be ignored.

The dashed line outlining a curved panel on the front of Template 2 applies only to Fireside Glow. The Twinkling Lights bag follows these instructions, but uses Template 3 instead of Template 2.

Follow instructions given with individual projects for all variations.

Bag lining

1 Cut the template along the dashed line to give a small top section (A) and large bottom section (B). Follow the steps for Bag Lining in Small Bag with Contrast Top, Darts, and Folded Handles (see pages 30–31).

Lined handles

1 Pin the fabric handle pieces to the appropriate pieces of interfacing: from this stage on, treat these two layers as one piece.

2 Along the long sides of each strip, press under ⅜ in. (1cm) and pin **(fig 1)**.

3 Press under ½ in. (12mm) along the long edges of the handle lining pieces.

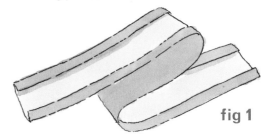

fig 1

4 With wrong sides together, pin each fabric handle to a lining, so that all the raw edges are concealed and the lining does not show on the right side **(fig 2)**. Set the sewing machine to medium straight stitch and, using matching sewing thread, topstitch close to the edges.

5 The handles can be attached to the bag following steps 4–6 of Folded Handles in Small Bag with Contrast Top, Darts, and Folded Handles (see page 30). Pin the handles to the bag with the lining facing outward.

Finishing

Follow the steps for Finishing in Small Bag with Contrast Top, Darts, and Folded Handles (see page 31).

Stitched-on handles

1 An alternative method for attaching the lined handles is done after the bag has been assembled: individual projects will suggest this method if appropriate. You will need to add 3 in. (8cm) to the length of each handle if you want to use this style of handle on any other bag. Trim each end of both handles, making sure that they are the same length.

2 Turn under $\frac{3}{8}$ in. (1cm) on each end of both handles. Pin the ends of each handle to the bag, 1½ in. (4cm) down from the top edge and aligned with the marks on the template **(fig 3)**.

3 Using the sewing machine, carefully sew the handles firmly in place. Topstitch a rectangle around the edges and then across the handle, in line with the top edge of the bag. Finish by stitching two decorative diagonal lines within the topstitched rectangle **(fig 4)**.

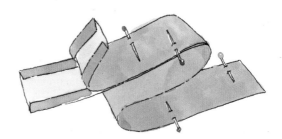

fig 2

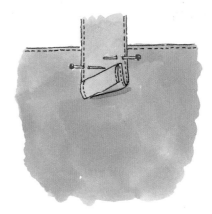

fig 3

fig 4

3: Medium bag with pleated top

Another bag that's the ideal size for carrying with you every day. This style has pleats that are stitched into a contrast top band to create fashionable shaping.

Projects using these instructions
• Lazy daisy (see pages 92–95)
• Button flowers (see pages 108–111)

Template 4 (see page 138)

Bag exterior

1 Enlarge both parts of Template 4 by 175 percent. We'll refer to the top section as A and the bottom section as B. In the same way as for step 2 of Small Bag with Contrast Top, Darts, and Folded Handles (see page 29), pin template B to the embroidered fabric. Add ⅜ in. (1cm) seam allowances and cut out the shape. Cut out the back of the bag using the same template and plain fabric.

2 Using the same template and adding seam allowances as for the embroidered fabric, cut out two pieces of interlining. Right side out, pin the bag front to one of the pieces of interlining: from this stage on, treat these two layers as one piece. Pin the bag back to the other piece of interlining and treat these layers as one piece also. Using a pencil, transfer the fold marks that are on the top edge of template B onto the back of the interlining.

3 Pin template A to the contrast top fabric. Add ⅜ in. (1cm) all around for seam allowances and cut out the shape twice. Using the same template and adding seam allowances as for the contrast fabric, cut out two pieces of interfacing. Right side out, pin each fabric piece to a piece of interfacing and treat the layers as one piece.

4 With right sides together and matching the side edges, pin the embroidered bag front to a contrast top piece. The embroidered piece will be wider than the top piece, so pin them together at the sides only **(fig 1)**.

5 On the back, pinch the top edge of the embroidered fabric at the marks transferred in step 2 to create two small pleats. Make sure the folds at the back of the pleats are facing toward the center of the bag and that the embroidered fabric is now lying flat against the contrast top. Pin the folds in place **(fig 2)**.

6 Following steps 4–5 of Bag Exterior in Small Bag with Contrast Top, Darts, and Folded Handles (see page 29), sew the embroidered and contrast top sections together, sewing the pleats in place as you do so **(fig 3)**. Assemble the bag back and top-stitch both pieces.

7 Following steps 9–10 of Bag Exterior in Small Bag with Contrast Top, Darts, and Folded Handles (see page 30), sew the bag front and back pieces together and mark the handle positions.

Folded handles

Follow the steps for Folded Handles in Small Bag with Contrast Top, Darts, and Folded Handles (see page 30).

Bag lining

Cut along the dashed lines on template B to make a template for the lining. Follow steps 1–3 and 5–7 of Bag Lining in Small Bag with Contrast Top, Darts, and Folded Handles (see pages 30–31) to assemble the lining and attach the magnetic clasp.

Finishing

Follow the steps for Finishing in Small Bag with Contrast Top, Darts, and Folded Handles (see page 31).

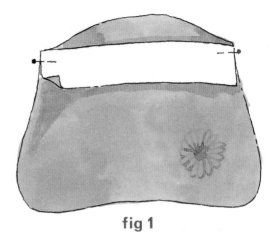

fig 1

fig 2

fig 3

Assembling a bag with a base

There are two versions of this type of bag. One version has a decorative, shaped top edge, the other has soft pleats to give extra roominess.

1: Bag with base and shaped top
2: Bag with base and top pleats

1: Bag with base and shaped top

This is a glamorous style of bag that will look fabulous on your arm on any occasion. It's also very practical, as the square base means that it'll easily carry all you need.

Projects using these instructions
- First bloom (see pages 44–47)
- Forest blooms (see pages 62–65)
- Les roses (see pages 68–71)

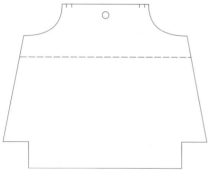

Template 5 (see page 139)

Bag exterior

1 Enlarge Template 5 by 202 percent. In the same way as for step 2 of Small Bag with Contrast Top, Darts, and Folded Handles (see page 29), pin the template to the embroidered fabric. Add ⅜ in. (1cm) seam allowances and cut out the shape using fabric scissors. Cut a bag back from plain fabric.

2 Using the same template and adding seam allowances as for the embroidered fabric, cut out two pieces of interlining. Right side out, pin the bag front to one of the pieces of interlining: from this stage on, treat these two layers as one piece. Pin the bag back to the other piece of interlining and treat these layers as one piece also.

3 Right sides together, pin the front and back pieces together down the sides and across the base, leaving open the inward corners at the bottom and the curved edge at the top. Set the sewing machine to a medium straight stitch. Taking a ⅜ in. (1cm) seam allowance, sew the side and base seams **(fig 1)**.

4 Flatten each inset corner so that the side seam touches the base seam and pin. Using the sewing machine and taking a ⅜ in. (1cm) seam allowance, sew across each corner **(fig 2)**. Make two lines of stitching for strength.

5 Referring to the template, lightly mark the handle positions on the front top edge of the bag with a pencil. Do the same on the back of the bag.

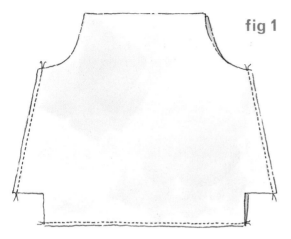

fig 1

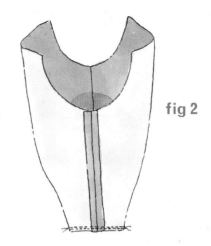

fig 2

Folded handles

Follow the steps for Folded Handles in Small Bag with Contrast Top, Darts, and Folded Handles (see page 30).

Bag lining

1 Cut along the dotted line on the template: the top section is for the facing and the bottom section for the lining. Follow steps 1–3 of Bag Lining in Small Bag with Contrast Top, Darts, and Folded Handles (see pages 30–31) to assemble the facing and lining **(fig 3)**.

2 Sew the front and back together and make the square corners as for steps 3–4 of Bag Exterior.

3 Finally, follow steps 6–7 of Bag Lining in Small Bag with Contrast Top, Darts, and Folded Handles (see page 31) to fit the magnetic clasp.

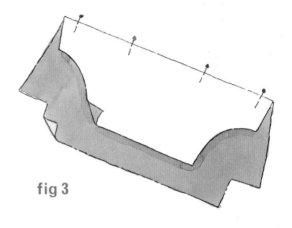

fig 3

Finishing

1 Follow steps 1–3 of Finishing in Small Bag with Contrast Top, Darts, and Folded Handles (see page 31).

2 Carefully insert the buckram base section through the opening between the handles **(fig 4)**. Make sure you push the base right into the corners at the bottom of the bag.

3 Turn in the seam allowances across the gap between the handles. Using a matching thread, topstitch around the top edge of the bag, sewing across the gap to close it.

fig 4

2: Bag with base and top pleats

This is the most capacious of all the styles of bag in this book. As well as a square base, it has pleats that are stitched into the contrast top band, making the body of the bag as large as possible.

Projects using these instructions
- Red hot (see pages 72–75)
- Fall blossoms (see pages 100–103)
- Sparkling leaves (see pages 122–125)

Template 6 (see page 140)

Bag exterior

1 Enlarge both parts of Template 6 by 223 percent. We'll refer to the top section as A and the bottom section as B. In the same way as for step 2 of Small Bag with Contrast Top, Darts, and Folded Handles (see page 29), pin template B to the embroidered fabric. Add ⅜ in. (1cm) seam allowances and cut out the shape using fabric scissors. Cut a bag back from plain fabric.

2 Using the same template and adding seam allowances as for the embroidered fabric, cut out two pieces of interlining. Right side out, pin the bag front to the one of the pieces of interlining: from this stage on, treat these two layers as one piece. Pin the bag back to the other piece of interlining and treat these layers as one piece also. Using a pencil, transfer the fold marks on the top edge of the template onto the back of the interlining.

3 On the back, pinch the top edge of the embroidered fabric at the marks transferred in step 2 to create six small pleats. Make sure the folds at the back of the pleats are all facing toward the center of the bag and pin then baste them in place **(fig 1)**.

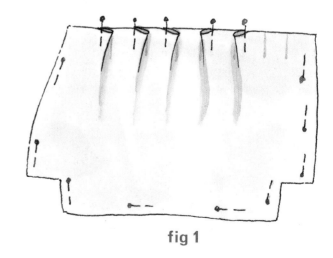

fig 1

4 Pin template A to the contrast top fabric. Add ⅜ in. (1cm) all around for seam allowances and cut out the shape twice using fabric scissors. Using the same template and adding seam allowances as for the contrast fabric, cut out two pieces of interfacing. Right side out, pin each contrast fabric piece to a piece of interfacing and treat the layers as one piece.

5 Following steps 4–5 of Bag Exterior in Small Bag with Contrast Top, Darts, and Folded Handles (see page 29), sew the embroidered and contrast top sections together, making sure they align at the sides and sewing the pleats in place as you do so **(fig 2)**. Remove the basting. Assemble the bag back and top-stitch both pieces.

6 Right sides together, pin the front and back pieces together down the sides and across the base, leaving open the top edge and the inset corners at the bottom **(fig 3)**. Set the sewing machine to a medium straight stitch. Taking a ⅜ in. (1cm) seam allowance, sew the side and base seams. Follow steps 4–5 of Bag Exterior in Bag with Base and Shaped Top (see page 36) to sew the corners and mark the handle positions.

Folded handles
Follow the steps for Folded Handles in Small Bag with Contrast Top, Darts, and Folded Handles (see page 30).

Bag lining
1 Cut along the dotted lines on template B to make a template for the lining. Follow steps 1–3 of Bag Lining in Small Bag with Contrast Top, Darts, and Folded Handles (see pages 30–31) to assemble the facing and lining

2 Sew the front and back together and make the square corners as for steps 3–4 of Bag Exterior in Bag with Base and Shaped Top (see page 36).

3 Finally, follow steps 6–7 of Bag Lining in Small Bag with Contrast Top, Darts, and Folded Handles (see page 31) to fit the magnetic clasp.

Finishing
1 Follow the steps for Finishing in Bag with Base and Shaped Top (see page 37). You can leave the buckram base out of the shoulder bags (as I did) if you prefer a softer look.

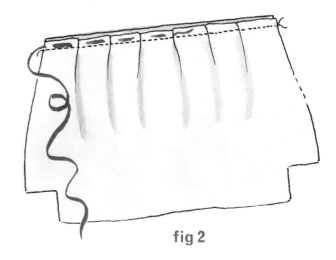

fig 2

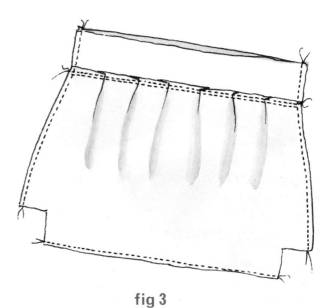

fig 3

Assembling a clutch bag

Both the clutch bags in this book are made in the same way. It's a straightforward style of bag to make as there are no handles to attach.

Clutch bag

Traditionally a classic evening bag shape, clutch bags are now also very fashionable as day bags. They don't hold a huge amount, but look so elegant that you'll forgive them and just carry less.

Projects using these instructions
• Sweet lavender (see pages 48–51)
• Verdant vine (see pages 104–107)

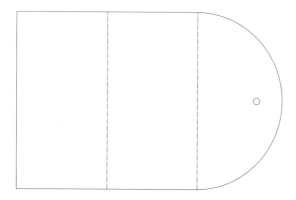

Template 7 (see page 141)

Bag exterior

1 Enlarge Template 7 by 218 percent. In the same way as for step 2 of Small Bag with Contrast Top, Darts, and Folded Handles (see page 29), pin the template to the embroidered fabric. Add ⅜ in. (1cm) seam allowances and cut out the shape using fabric scissors.

2 Pin the same template to the interfacing. Add seam allowances as for the embroidered fabric and cut out the shape. With a pencil, mark the dotted fold lines on the back of the interfacing.

3 Right side out, pin the fabric to the interfacing: from this stage on, treat these two layers as one piece.

4 Right sides together, fold the bag at the first dotted fold line and pin the sides together. Set the sewing machine to a medium straight stitch. Taking a ⅜ in. (1cm) seam allowance, sew the side seams **(fig 1)**.

Bag lining

1 Pin the template to the lining fabric. Add ⅜ in. (1cm) seam allowances all around and cut out the shape using fabric scissors.

2 Cut along the second dotted line on the template, cutting off the curved flap section. Discard the rest of the template. Pin the flap template to the flap interfacing and cut out the shape.

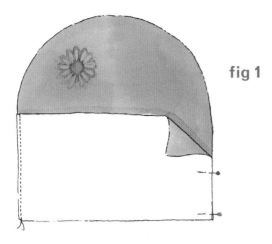

fig 1

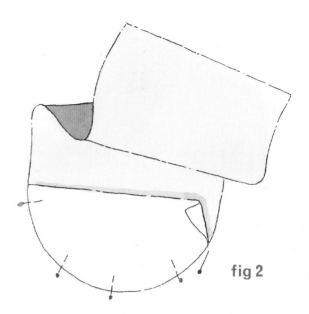

fig 2

3 Lay the flap section of interfacing on the flap section of the wrong isde of the lining fabric and pin the layers together around the curved edge **(fig 2)**.

4 Following step 4 of Bag Exterior, fold the lining and sew the side seams. Following step 6 of Bag Lining in Small Bag with Contrast Top, Darts, and Folded Handles (see page 31), attach one half of the magnetic clasp to the right side of the interfaced flap of the lining, in the position marked on the template.

Finishing

1 With right sides together and matching the side seams, put the embroidered bag inside the lining. Pin the layers together around the edges.

2 Set the sewing machine to a medium straight stitch. Starting at the front edge, sew all the way around the front edge and the flap, leaving an opening of approximately 6 in. (15cm) at center front **(fig 3)**. You may need to cut two small notches at each of the side seams to allow you to ease the fabric in a straight line through the sewing machine. Turn the bag right side out.

3 Following step 7 of Bag Lining in Small Bag with Contrast Top, Darts, and Folded Handles (see page 31), attach the other half of the magnetic clasp to the front of the bag. Reach through the opening in the stitching to fold the prongs flat. Take care to ensure that the halves of the clasp are properly positioned so that when the bag flap is closed, it lies flat.

4 Turn in the seam allowances across the gap. Using a matching thread, topstitch around the front edge and flap of the bag, sewing across the gap to close it **(fig 4)**.

fig 3

fig 4

Spring bags

My Spring collection features bags with a fresh, optimistic color palette and delicate embroidery to herald the new buds and emerging foliage of the season. The shapes are practical for daily use, and the designs so pretty that you can carry your bag with confidence at formal or casual occasions. A spring wedding might see you with Sweet Lavender or Bow and Bouquet, while a lovely long lunch with girlfriends might be an ideal outing for First Bloom.

First bloom

This beautiful cream springtime bag is a real statement piece. I have chosen dramatic scarlet lace to embroider the vibrant red, poppy-style flower, adding texture and an interesting creative dimension. I have used a rich chocolate brown lace for the larger leaves, which is echoed in the oversized chocolate brown button and the sequin flower center. The fine wool embroidered leaves, in graduating shades from lime green to intense olive, keep the whole look fresh and exciting.

STITCHES USED
- **Satin stitch**
- **Running stitch**
- **Fishbone stitch**
- **Straight stitch**

Materials

18 x 27½ in. (45 x 70cm) of heavyweight, textured, cream wool fabric for bag

18 x 27½ in. (45 x 70cm) of heavyweight, woven interlining for bag

14 x 4¾ in. (35 x 12cm) of heavyweight, chocolate brown brushed cotton for handles

14 x 4¾ in. (35 x 12cm) of medium-weight, sew-in interfacing for handles

15¼ x 9½ in. (38 x 24cm) of heavyweight, textured, cream wool fabric for facing

15¼ x 9½ in. (38 x 24cm) of heavyweight, sew-in interfacing for facing

18 x 20 in. (45 x 50cm) of cream cotton lining fabric for bag

11 x 4 in. (28 x 10cm) of heavyweight buckram for base

Lace approx ⅜ in. (1cm) wide in scarlet, chocolate brown, and coffee brown

Strong sewing thread in a dark color

Vintage button in yellow

Sequins in chocolate brown

Fine wool yarn in chocolate brown, sable brown, and three or four graduating shades of green from lime to deep olive

Sewing threads to match the textured cream and chocolate brown fabrics

Magnetic clasp

Oversized button in chocolate brown

Equipment

Template 5 (see page 139)

Fabric scissors

Long dressmaker's pins

Pencil

Large embroidery hoop

Darning needle

Small embroidery scissors

Fine sewing needle

Embroidery needles in varying sizes

Ruler

Iron

Sewing machine

First bloom

1 ▲ **Enlarge Template 5** by the amount stated and cut out the shape to make a paper pattern. Pin the pattern to the textured, cream fabric and draw around it, adding ¾ in. (2cm) for seam allowance and fabric shrinkage. Remove the pattern. Using the pencil, lightly draw out the design, using the main photograph as a guide. Fit the fabric into the embroidery hoop (see page 16).

2 ▲ **Using the darning needle** and the scarlet lace, embroider the flower in satin stitch, stitching one petal at a time until all the petals have been completed.

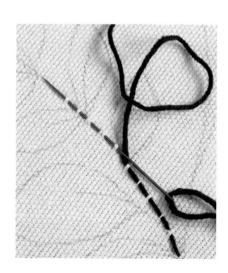

3 ▲ **Using the strong thread,** sew the antique yellow button into the center of the flower.

4 ▲ **To finish off** the flower center, sew on chocolate brown sequins around the button, making sure you keep them tightly packed.

5 ▲ **With the chocolate brown** yarn, sew lines of running stitch for the stems.

6 ▲ **Using the darning needle** and the chocolate brown lace, embroider the lower large leaf at the base of the stem in fishbone stitch. Embroider the other large leaf with the coffee brown lace.

7 ▲ **Using the green yarns,** and beginning with the lightest color at the tip of each sprig, embroider the smaller leaves in fishbone stitch. Once you have stitched about four leaves, change to a slightly darker shade of green yarn and embroider the next few. Finish embroidering with the darkest olive green at the base of each sprig. With the sable brown yarn, embroider three straight stitches at the base of each leaf.

8 ◄ **Remove the fabric** from the embroidery hoop and assemble the bag following the instructions for Bag with Base and Shaped Top (see pages 36–37). To finish, sew on the chocolate brown oversized button to the center top of the bag front.

Sweet lavender

STITCHES USED
- **French knot**
- **Backstitch**
- **Straight stitch**
- **Fishbone stitch**

This simple, elegant clutch bag in the palest pewter-colored dupioni silk fabric, is a truly timeless purse. The delicate lavender sprigs are made from French knots in lavender, cotton ribbon yarn and are embellished with silver beads and tiny lavender-purple seed beads. Edged with large, matte-silver, square sequins and finished with a couple of diamond-shaped, faded-violet glass beads, this is a classic bag that will last a lifetime.

Materials
22 x 15¼ in. (55 x 38cm) of pale, pewter-colored, dupioni silk

22 x 15¼ in. (55 x 38cm) of heavyweight sew-in interfacing

22 x 15¼ in. (55 x 38cm) of cream cotton lining fabric

15¼ x 8 in. (38 x 20cm) of heavyweight sew-in interfacing for bag flap

Cotton ribbon yarn in lavender

Strong sewing thread in a neutral color

Small beads in silver

Tiny seed beads in lavender

Shiny rayon floss in grass green and purple

Sewing threads to match dupioni silk and cream lining fabric

Magnetic clasp

Square sequins in matte-silver

Selection of glass beads in silver and faded violet

Equipment
Template 7 (see page 141)

Fabric scissors

Long dressmaker's pins

Pencil

Large embroidery hoop

Embroidery needles in varying sizes

Fine beading needle

Small embroidery scissors

Ruler

Iron

Sewing machine

Fine sewing needle

Sweet lavender

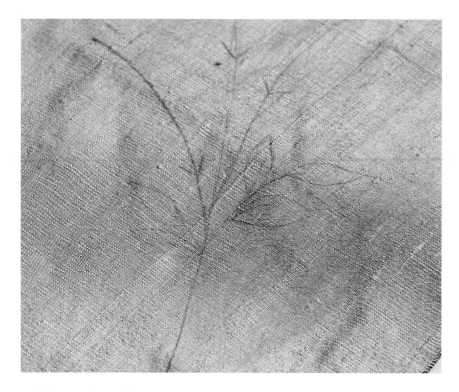

1 ◀ **Enlarge Template 7** by the amount stated and cut out the shape to make a paper pattern. Pin the pattern to the pewter-colored silk fabric and draw around it, adding ¾ in. (2cm) for seam allowance and fabric shrinkage. Remove the pattern. Using the pencil, lightly draw out the design, using the main photograph as a guide and indicating the flowering lavender sprigs with just a faint single central line. Fit the fabric into the embroidery hoop (see page 16).

2 ▲ **Using the lavender yarn** and starting at the tip of each sprig, embroider the flower heads in French knots. Work your way down the lavender stem, making the knots close together. Continue until a lovely, lavender-shaped flower sprig has been formed.

3 ▲ **To add detail** to the sprigs, use the strong sewing thread to sew on silver beads, one at a time, in between the French knots. Place them wherever you think they are needed to enhance the flower. Next, sew tiny lavender seed beads to the sprigs, again in between the French knots.

4 ▲ **Cut a length** of the grass green rayon floss and separate the strands into two groups. This gives you two finer lengths of floss to embroider with instead of one thicker length.

5 ◀ **Starting at the base** of one of the sprigs, embroider the fine central stem in backstitch. Repeat for the other flower stems. Create tiny leaves by sewing three straight stitches on either side of the stem, just below the flower heads.

6 ▶ **Embroider the delicate** leaves in fishbone stitch. To add detail to these leaves, take a single strand of the purple rayon floss and sew a single straight stitch at the base of each leaf.

7 ◀ **Remove the fabric** from the embroidery hoop and assemble the bag following the instructions for Clutch Bag (see pages 40–41). When the assembly is complete, sew a line of matte-silver square sequins around the edge of the flap using the strong sewing thread. Position a sequin, take the needle down through the hole, make a small stitch through the silk fabric only, and bring the needle up again at the edge of the sequin. Take the needle down again though the hole and up again where it last came out (see inset). Sew on each sequin in this way.

8 ▲ **Lastly, create the** clasp trim by threading several of the silver beads and violet glass beads onto strong sewing thread. Stitch through the center of the flap edge. Repeat to make two small beaded tassels.

Bow and bouquet

STITCHES USED
- **Spider's web stitch**
- **Daisy stitch**
- **Fishbone stitch**
- **Straight stitch**
- **Running stitch**
- **Detached chain stitch**

This gorgeous little bag is made in pale olive green dupioni silk and is finished with a contrasting rich raspberry red silk top band and elegant bow. The delicate embroidery—done with pink lace and wool yarns of different weights—and the long tails of the trailing bow all add a sumptuous feel, a real sense of occasion. This bag is the perfect accessory for any springtime event, whether it's a night at the opera, a wonderful wedding, or a relaxed drinks evening with friends.

Materials

14 x 18 in. (35 x 45cm) of pale olive green dupioni silk for bag

14 x 20 in. (35 x 50cm) of heavyweight, woven interlining for bag

12 x 6¼ in. (30 x 16cm) of raspberry red dupioni silk for contrast top band

14 x 3 in. (35 x 8cm) of pale olive green dupioni silk for handles

14 x 3 in. (35 x 8cm) of medium-weight, sew-in interfacing for handles

14 x 16 in. (35 x 40cm) of vibrant pink satin lining fabric for bag

12 x 6¼ in. (30 x 16cm) of raspberry red dupioni silk for facing

12 x 6¼ in. (30 x 16cm) of medium-weight, sew-in interfacing for facing

31½ x 4 in. (80 x 10cm) of raspberry red dupioni silk for bow

Embroidery floss in pink

Lace approx ⅜ in. (1cm) wide in bubblegum pink

Thick wool yarn in pale lavender

Strong sewing thread in a neutral color

Small beads in antique gold

Fine wool yarn in deep olive green and ecru

Sewing threads to match silk and lining fabrics

Magnetic clasp

Equipment

Template 1 (see page 135)

Fabric scissors

Long dressmaker's pins

Pencil

Large embroidery hoop

Embroidery needles in varying sizes

Embroidery scissors

Darning needle

Beading needle

Ruler

Iron

Sewing machine

Fine sewing needle

Bow and bouquet

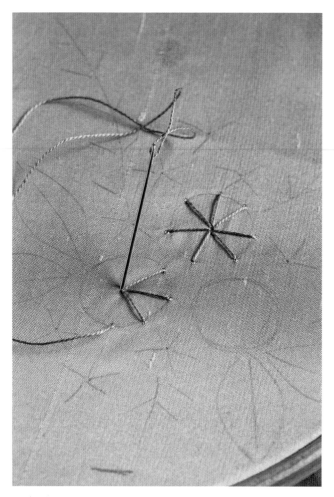

1 ▲ **Enlarge Template 1** by the amount stated and cut out the section below the horizontal dotted line to make a paper pattern. Pin the pattern to the green silk fabric and draw around it, adding ¾ in. (2cm) for seam allowance and fabric shrinkage. Remove the pattern. Using the pencil, lightly draw out the design, using the main photograph as a guide. Fit the fabric into the embroidery hoop (see page 16). Using the pink embroidery floss, stitch the seven spokes of the spider's web for each flower.

2 ▲ **Using the bubblegum pink** lace and the darning needle, fill in the spider's webs. Starting at the center, pass the needle over and under the spokes, making sure you keep the lace taut as you work. Gradually build up each flower until all the spokes have been completely covered (see inset).

3 ▲ **Embroider the small** flowers in daisy stitch, making five petals for each flower with the lavender yarn.

4 ▲ **Sew a gold** bead into the center of each of the lavender daisies using the strong sewing thread.

5 ◄ **Using the deep** olive green yarn, embroider the large leaves in fishbone stitch. Finish each one with three small straight stitches in ecru yarn to add detail.

Sewing on beads

You can use specialist beading thread—rather than strong sewing thread—to sew on beads, but bear in mind that beading thread is available only in a limited range of colors. I use strong sewing thread and have always found this to be successful. You can wax the thread if you wish, but don't over-wax or it will mark the silk.

▶

Bow and bouquet

6 ▲ **Again using the** olive green yarn, embroider the stems of the leafy sprigs in running stitch. Starting at the top of each sprig and using the detached chain stitch, sew tiny individual leaves to complete the embroidery. Remove the fabric from the embroidery hoop and assemble the bag following the instructions for Small Bag with Contrast Top, Darts, and Folded Handles (see pages 28–31).

7 ▲ **Right sides together**, fold the long strip of raspberry red dupioni silk in half lengthways. Using the sewing machine, sew around the raw edges taking a ⅜ in. (1cm) seam allowance and leaving a 4 in. (10cm) gap in the center of the long edge. Sew across the short ends at an angle, as shown.

8 ▶ **Trim off excess fabric** at the short ends. Turn the strip right side out through the gap. Turn under the seam allowances across the gap, slip stitch it closed and iron the strip.

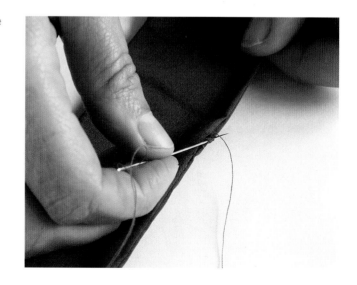

9 ◀ **Tie the strip** into a bow, leaving the tail ends long.

10 ▶ **Using matching sewing** thread, carefully sew the bow onto the contrast band at the top of the bag, making small stitches through the back of the knot.

Variation

This little bag is made from the same pale olive green silk, but without the contrast top edge. To make this version, use the whole of the template as the pattern piece and ignore Steps 2–5 of Bag Exterior in the assembly instructions. The pert bow is made in raspberry silk in the same way as the bow for the Sparkling Leaves bag (see page 122). The embroidery consists of the lavender daisies and green leaves only.

Pink and pretty

Made in vibrant, pink linen fabric, this bag encompasses a whole variety of embroidery techniques and beaded detailing. There is a combination of textures, flosses, and wools, from the palest pink mohair to shimmering lilac rayon, from the richest of deep plum-colored fine threads to variegated, colorful viscose fibers. Mixing and matching flosses adds interest, so be creative and source as many different types as you can. Keeping to one color palette will bring it all together.

STITCHES USED
- **Spider's web stitch**
- **Running stitch**
- **Fishbone stitch**
- **Daisy stitch**
- **Detached chain stitch**

Materials
16 x 12 in. (40 x 30cm) of vibrant pink linen fabric for bag front

16 x 12 in. (40 x 30cm) of brick red linen fabric for bag back

16 x 24 in. (40 x 60cm) of heavyweight, woven interlining for bag

18 x 4 in. (45 x 10cm) of brick red linen fabric for handles

18 x 4 in. (45 x 10cm) of medium-weight, sew-in interfacing for handles

18 x 4 in. (45 x 10cm) of bright pink satin lining for handles

14 x 5½ in. (35 x 14cm) of brick red linen for facing

14 x 5½ in. (35 x 14cm) of heavyweight, sew-in interfacing for facing

16 x 20 in. (40 x 50cm) of bright pink satin lining

Variegated fine embroidery floss in deep red/plum

Variegated viscose cord in magenta/crimson/rose red

Glittery crimson woven yarn

Strong sewing thread in a neutral color

Pearl beads with an antique finish

Cotton ribbon yarn in fuchsia

Pearlized beads in deep black currant

Rayon ribbon yarn in pale lilac and muted rose

Seed beads in antique silver, pale pink, ruby red, and muted lilac

Pale pink mohair wool

Baby pink wool yarn

Sewing threads to match linen and lining fabrics

Magnetic clasp

Equipment
Template 2 (see page 136)

Fabric scissors

Long dressmaker's pins

Pencil

Large embroidery hoop

Embroidery needles in varying sizes

Small embroidery scissors

Darning needle

Fine beading needle

Ruler

Iron

Sewing machine

Pink and pretty

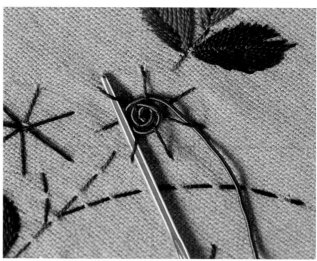

1 ▲ **Enlarge Template 2** by the amount stated and cut out the shape to make a paper pattern. Pin the pattern to the pink linen and draw around it, adding ¾ in. (2cm) for seam allowance and fabric shrinkage. Remove the pattern. Using the pencil, lightly draw out the design, using the main photograph as a guide. Fit the fabric into the embroidery hoop (see page 16). Using the variegated embroidery floss, sew the seven spokes of each spider's web. Continuing in the same floss, embroider all the stems in running stitch and the leaves in fishbone stitch.

2 ▲ **Using the variegated** viscose cord and a darning needle, fill in the spider's webs. Starting at the center, pass the cord over and under alternate spokes until they are covered and a beautiful rose shape has been formed.

3 ◄ **Working methodically across** the fabric, embroider two stems of daisies in the glittery crimson yarn. Starting at the tip of each stem, sew one stitch for each bud, three stitches for each budding flower and five stitches for each main flower. Sew a pearl bead into the center of each main flower using the strong sewing thread. Embroider the third stem in the fuchsia yarn, sewing a black currant bead into the centers of the flowers.

4 ► **Using the lilac** rayon yarn and detached chain stitch, embroider one group of leaf sprigs. Embroider the other group using the rose rayon yarn. Sew on a pale pink seed bead at the tip of each leaf.

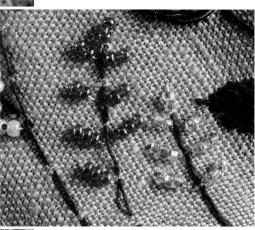

5 ◀ **Using the strong** sewing thread, sew on groups of three lilac seed beads on either side of some of the smaller sprigs. Repeat on the remaining sprigs, using the antique silver, ruby red, and pale pink beads (see inset).

6 ◀ **Using the pale pink** mohair yarn, embroider two of the larger flowers and the two budding flowers in daisy stitch. Use the baby pink yarn to embroider the remaining larger flower.

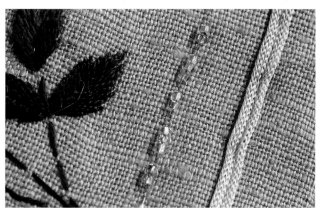

7 ▲ **Sew on a broken** line of silver seed beads at the base of the design, attaching two or three at a time. Take the fabric out of the hoop and, using the sewing machine, sew on a length of the pale lilac rayon under the beads. Assemble the bag following the instructions for Medium Bag with Darts and Lined Handles (see pages 32–33). Sew the handles on after assembling the bag.

Forest blooms

STITCHES USED
- **Running stitch**
- **Straight stitch**
- **Fishbone stitch**
- **Daisy stitch**
- **Satin stitch**
- **Detached chain stitch**
- **Spider's web stitch**

This elegant, aqua blue linen bag is embroidered with an array of fine, green woolen yarns—from the fairest of fern greens, through to avocado, grass green, and rich olive—mixed with sparkling sepia, turquoise blue, and taupe rayon fibers. The bag is finished with large, pearlized, apple green and chocolate brown beads, flat, aqua sequins and an antique gold filigree button. The zesty color palette balances the delicate embroidery beautifully.

Materials

18 x 27½ in. (45 x 70cm) of aqua linen fabric for bag

18 x 27½ in. (45 x 70cm) of thick woven interlining for bag

14 x 4¾ in. (35 x 12cm) of pale aqua linen for handles

14 x 4¾ in. (35 x 12cm) of medium-weight, sew-in interfacing for handles

15¼ x 9½ in. (38 x 24cm) of aqua linen fabric for facing

15¼ x 9½ in. (38 x 24cm) of heavyweight, sew-in interfacing for facing

18 x 20 in. (45 x 50cm) of cream cotton lining fabric

11 x 4 in. (28 x 10cm) of thick buckram for base

Fine wool yarns in apple green, pale fern, grass green, and rich olive green

Strong sewing thread in a neutral color

Large pearlized beads in rich chocolate brown and apple green

Variegated cotton ribbon yarn in green/aqua

Sparkly rayon yarn in sepia

Rayon ribbon yarn in taupe, turquoise, and sky blue

Tiny seed beads in antique silver

Variegated chenille yarn in pale fern/apple green

Sewing threads to match the aqua linens and cream cotton fabrics

Magnetic clasp

Small, flat sequins in aqua

Large antique gold button

Equipment

Template 5 (see page 139)

Fabric scissors

Long dressmaker's pins

Pencil

Large embroidery hoop

Embroidery needles in varying sizes

Small embroidery scissors

Fine beading needle

Darning needle

Ruler

Iron

Sewing machine

Fine sewing needle

Forest blooms

1 ◀ **Enlarge Template 5** by the amount stated and cut out the shape to make a paper pattern. Pin the pattern to the aqua linen and draw around it, adding ¾ in. (2cm) for seam allowance and fabric shrinkage. Remove the pattern. Using the pencil, lightly draw out the design, using the main photograph as a guide. Fit the fabric into the embroidery hoop (see page 16). Using the rich olive yarn, embroider the main stems, including all the sprigs, with simple running stitch. Sew tiny leaves and a base for each of the budding daisies with a few straight stitches. With the same yarn, embroider a few of the leaves in fishbone stitch. Then embroider the remaining leaves, also using fishbone stitch, with the pale fern, apple green, and grass green yarns.

2 ▶ **Using the apple green yarn** and working in daisy stitch, embroider the two large daisies and two budding flowers. Sew a chocolate brown bead into the center of each daisy using the strong sewing thread.

3 ▲ **With the variegated** green/aqua cotton ribbon yarn, embroider the smaller flowers in satin stitch, sewing three or four stitches for each petal. Sew an apple green pearlized bead into the center of each flower.

4 ◀ **Using the sparkling** rayon yarn in sepia and detached chain stitch, sew tiny leaves on a section of stem. Fill the remaining sprigs with the same leaves, but using the taupe, turquoise, and sky blue rayon ribbon yarns. Sew a silver seed bead to the tip of each leaf (see inset).

5 ◀ **Using the pale** fern yarn, stitch the seven spokes of the spider's web on the three remaining flowers. Using the darning needle, fill in the spider's webs with the chenille yarn, going over and under each spoke until they are all covered.

6 ▲ **Remove the fabric** from the embroidery hoop and assemble the bag following the instructions for Bag with Base and Shaped Top (see pages 36–37). When the assembly is complete, sew a line of aqua sequins around the top edge of the bag. Position a sequin, take the needle down through the hole in the middle, and make a small stitch through the top layer of fabric. Take the needle down again though the middle of the sequin and up again where it last came out. Sew on each sequin in this way (see also step 7 of Sweet Lavender, page 51).

7 ▲ **Finally, sew the** antique gold decorative button to the center top of the bag front.

Summer bags

Celebrate the season with masses of blossoms in gorgeous colors and sumptuous textiles, courtesy of my Summer collection of embroidered bags. There are bags with big, bold blooms in rich colors and textured yarns, and bags with delicate flowers in pastel silk ribbon or fabric. You might want a colorful and capacious bag for your summer vacation, or a smart but feminine accessory for a party, or simply a daily use bag that makes every outfit feel special.

Les roses

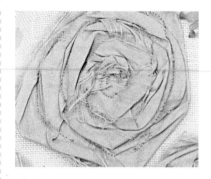

STITCHES USED
- **Daisy stitch**
- **Fishbone stitch**

The inspiration for Les Roses came directly from a treasured book by Pierre-Joseph Redouté, whose beautiful flower and plant illustrations offer endless inspiration for embroidery and appliqué. By twisting and stitching strips of pale pink dupioni silk to form elegant flower heads, I created soft texture to complement the embroidered leaves in pale pewter cotton yarn and delicate, pale pink daisy flowers worked in organza ribbon.

Materials
18 x 14 in. (45 x 35cm) of white linen fabric for bag front

18 x 14 in. (45 x 35cm) of ecru linen fabric in neutral for bag back

35½ x 14 in. (90 x 35cm) of heavyweight, woven interlining for bag

14 x 4¾ in. (35 x 12cm) of ecru linen fabric in neutral for handles

14 x 4¾ in. (35 x 12cm) of medium-weight, sew-in interfacing for handles

15¼ x 9½ in. (38 x 24cm) of natural linen fabric in neutral for facing

15¼ x 9½ in. (38 x 24cm) of heavyweight, sew-in interfacing for facing

18 x 20 in. (45 x 50cm) of deep pink cotton lining fabric

11 x 4 in. (28 x 10cm) of heavyweight buckram for base

20 x 20 in. (50 x 50cm) of pale pink dupioni silk

Sewing thread to match the white and neutral linen fabrics, the deep pink lining, and the pale pink dupioni silk

100 in. (250cm) of ⅜ in. (1cm) wide organza ribbon in pale pink

Strong sewing thread in a neutral color

Pearlized beads in champagne color

Seed beads in antique silver

Cotton ribbon yarn in pale pewter

Small sequins in pearlized pink

Flat sequins in dusky, pale pink

Magnetic clasp

Equipment
Template 5 (see page 139)

Fabric scissors

Long dressmaker's pins

Pencil

Large embroidery hoop

Embroidery scissors

Sewing machine

Embroidery needles in varying sizes

Fine sewing needle

Beading needle

Ruler

Iron

Les roses

1 **Enlarge Template 5** by the amount stated and cut out the shape to make a paper pattern. Pin the pattern to the white linen fabric and draw around it, adding ¾ in. (2cm) for seam allowance and fabric shrinkage. Remove the pattern. Using the pencil, lightly draw out the design, using the main photograph as a guide. Indicate where the rose flowers will be by drawing circles.

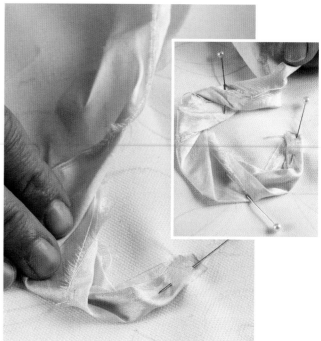

2 ▲ **Tear the pale pink** dupioni silk into strips, each one measuring approximately 2 x 20 in. (5 x 50cm). Pull off any loose threads so each strip has soft, slightly frayed edges.

3 ▲ **Fold one end** of a strip in half and in half again and pin it to the outer edge of one of the drawn rose circles. Begin loosely twisting the strip, winding it around the circle and pinning it in place as you go. Continue in concentric circles, each one slightly overlapping the previous one, winding the fabric toward the center of the flower.

4 ▲ **When you reach** the center of the flower, cut off any excess fabric and tuck in the end, securing it with a pin. Try to twist the fabric a little more as you get nearer the center to create a natural rose effect.

5 ◀ **Fit the fabric** into the embroidery hoop, making sure that it is flush with the bottom of the hoop and not the top, as is usual. Remove the presser foot from the sewing machine or fit a free-motion embroidery foot, whichever is used with your machine. Set the machine to straight stitch and drop the feed dog (the manual for your sewing machine will tell you how to do this). Put the embroidery hoop under the needle so that the fabric lies flat on the bed of the machine. Starting at the outside edge, sew the first rose onto the linen, gently moving the hoop in a spiral motion until the stitching ends up in the center of the flower. Sew on each rose in this way.

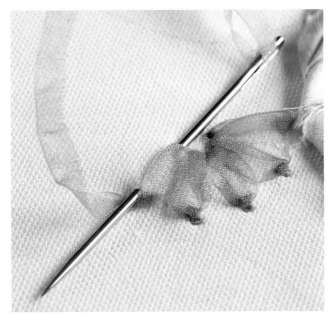

6 ▲ **Take the fabric** out of the hoop and fit it back in again in the usual way (see page 16). Using the pale pink organza ribbon, embroider the remaining flowers with daisy stitch.

7 ▲ **Using the strong** sewing thread, sew a pearlized bead into the center of each daisy to add detail. Sewing on two beads at a time, stitch on a ring of silver seed beads around each pearl.

8 ▲ **Using the pale** pewter yarn, embroider the leaves with fishbone stitch.

9 ▲ **Following step 7** of Sweet Lavender (see page 51), sew on the pearlized and flat sequins, scattering them over the design wherever you think they are needed.

10 ▲ **Remove the fabric** from the embroidery hoop and assemble the bag following the instructions for Bag with Base and Shaped Top (see pages 36–37). To finish, sew on a line of pale pink, flat sequins around the top edge of the bag.

Red hot

This large bag is just the thing to accompany any outfit, either casual or smart, on a sizzling summer day. The fine netting I have used for the oversized embroidered flowers is set off perfectly by the fiery red, textured linen fabric. Edged with rich, chocolate brown linen, the bag is finished off with a large pink button.

STITCHES USED
- **Satin stitch**
- **French knot**
- **Daisy stitch**
- **Fishbone stitch**

Materials

22 x 24 in. (55 x 60cm) of red, textured linen for bag

22 x 24 in. (55 x 60cm) of heavyweight, woven interlining for bag

14 x 12¾ in. (35 x 32cm) of chocolate brown linen for contrast top band

14 x 12¾ in. (35 x 32cm) of heavyweight, sew-in interfacing for contrast top band

14 x 4¾ in. (35 x 12cm) of chocolate brown linen for handles

14 x 4¾ in. (35 x 12cm) of medium-weight, sew-in interfacing for handles

22 x 24 in. (55 x 60cm) of peach cotton lining fabric

4 x 14½ in. (10 x 36cm) of heavyweight buckram for base

Fine netting in ecru, cut into long strips measuring approximately 1½ in. (4cm) wide

Thick wool in dark eggplant color and bubblegum pink

Two small mother-of-pearl shirt buttons

Strong sewing thread in a neutral color

Pearlized beads

Cotton ribbon yarn in lilac and pale olive green

Sequins in tea-rose and lilac

Sewing threads to match the red and brown linens and the peach lining fabric

Magnetic clasp

One large pink button

Equipment

Template 6 (see page 140)

Fabric scissors

Long dressmaker's pins

Pencil

Large embroidery hoop

Large darning needle

Embroidery scissors

Embroidery needles in varying sizes

Fine sewing needle

Beading needle

Ruler

Iron

Sewing machine

Red hot

1 ▶ **Enlarge Template 6** by the amount stated and cut out the main bag section to make a paper pattern. Pin the pattern to the red linen fabric and draw around it, adding ¾ in. (2cm) for seam allowance and fabric shrinkage. Remove the pattern. Using the pencil, lightly draw out the design, using the main photograph as a guide. Fit the fabric into the embroidery hoop (see page 16). Using the large darning needle and the netting strips, embroider the large flowers in satin stitch.

2 ▲ **Using the eggplant-colored wool**, embroider a ring of tightly packed French knots around the edge of the flower center.

3 ▲ **Finish off the flowers** by sewing a shirt button into the center of each one.

4 ▲ **Using the bubblegum pink** yarn, embroider the smaller flowers in daisy stitch.

5 ▶ **Sew a pearlized bead** into the center of each daisy. Embroider the smallest flowers in lilac yarn and daisy stitch and sew a sequin into the middle of each one. Sew on more sequins, scattering them on the red linen wherever you feel they are needed.

6 ▲ **Using the pale olive green** yarn, embroider all of the leaves with fishbone stitch to complete the design.

7 ▲ **Remove the fabric** from the hoop and assemble the bag following the instructions for Bag with Base and Top Pleats (see pages 38–39). To finish, sew the pink button to the center top of the bag front.

Wildflower days

STITCHES USED
- **Daisy stitch**
- **Running stitch**
- **Fishbone stitch**
- **Satin stitch**

This bag features an assortment of dainty wild flowers worked in fine yarns and threads, including mohair, metallic fibers, and delicate wools and cottons. Metallic sequins, striking green velvet trim, and a large, mother-of-pearl square button complete the look. Most of the yarns I have used are found remnants and treasured samples I have kept and collected over the years, waiting for the right project in which to use them.

Materials

16 x 24 in. (40 x 60cm) of turquoise linen fabric for bag

16 x 24 in. (40 x 60cm) of heavyweight, woven interlining for bag

12 x 4¾ in. (30 x 12cm) of royal blue linen fabric for handles

12 x 4¾ in. (30 x 12cm) of medium-weight, sew-in interfacing for handles

14 x 5½ in. (35 x 14cm) of turquoise linen for facing

14 x 5½ in. (35 x 14cm) of heavyweight, sew-in interfacing for facing

16 x 20 in. (40 x 50cm) of royal blue cotton lining fabric

Mohair yarn in pale blue

Strong sewing thread in a neutral color

Beads in pearlized green and metallic brown

Cotton floss in vivid blue

Crimped wool in pale yellow

Sparkly metallic yarn in green/gold

Thick, woven cotton ribbon yarn in peach/brown

Variegated cotton yarn in blue/green

Fine wool yarn in bright turquoise

A selection of fine wool yarns in pale, mid-tone, and glittery greens

Seed beads in gold and silver

Sewing threads to match the turquoise linen, royal blue linen, lining fabric, and green velvet ribbon

39 in. (100cm) strip of sequins in peacock blue

27½ in. (70cm) of narrow velvet ribbon in bright green

Magnetic clasp

Large, square mother-of-pearl button

Equipment

Template 2 (see page 136)

Fabric scissors

Long dressmaker's pins

Pencil

Large embroidery hoop

Embroidery needles in varying sizes

Embroidery scissors

Fine beading needle

Ruler

Iron

Sewing machine

Fine sewing needle

Wildflower days

1 ◀ **Enlarge Template 2** by the amount stated and cut out the whole shape to make a paper pattern. Pin the pattern to the turquoise linen fabric and draw around it, adding ¾ in. (2cm) for seam allowance and fabric shrinkage. Remove the pattern. Using the pencil, lightly draw out the design, using the main photograph as a guide. Fit the fabric into the embroidery hoop (see page 16). Using the pale blue mohair yarn, embroider three flowers in daisy stitch. Sew a green pearlized bead into the middle of each one. Using the vivid blue floss, sew the stems in running stitch and the leaves in fishbone stitch.

2 ▲ **Using daisy stitch** again, embroider the pale yellow flowers with the crimped yarn. Stitch only five or six petals on a couple of the top flowers, which will give a more natural impression of the flowers budding. Sew the stems and leaves as for step 1 and the bases of the budding flowers with four or five satin stitches.

3 ▶ **Embroider the remaining** smaller flowers in daisy stitch with the unused metallic yarns and variegated cotton threads. Embroider stems, leaves, and bases as before, using the green yarns.

4 ▲ **Sew gold or silver** seed beads into the centers of all the tiny, open flowers. Remove the fabric from the embroidery hoop.

5 ▲ **Measure approximately** 1¼ in. (3cm) up from the bottom edge of the bag front and, with the ruler, draw faint horizontal lines in pencil. Lay a strip of sequins along this line and sew one end in place with a few hand stitches. Make sure the sequins overlap in the same direction the presser foot faces: If they overlap toward it this will make sewing them on more difficult. Set the sewing machine to a medium straight stitch. Holding the line of sequins taut in front of the needle, sew slowly along it. The shiny sequins are slippery, so be careful the needle doesn't slip.

6 ◀ **Using the line of sequins** as a guide, pin a length of the velvet ribbon just below it. Using matching thread, sew down one edge of the ribbon. Starting at the same end, sew down the other edge. Repeat steps 5–6 at the top of the bag, sewing on a line of sequins either side of the velvet ribbon.

7 ◀ **Assemble the bag** following the instructions for Medium Bag with Darts and Lined Handles (see pages 32–33), but substituting the folded handles from page 30. To finish, sew the mother-of-pearl button to the center top of the bag front.

Garden fresh

STITCHES USED
- **Running stitch**
- **Detached chain stitch**
- **French knot**
- **Backstitch**

This stylish, elegant summer bag in the darkest of navy blue linens is simply exquisite. Incorporating delicate, embroidered silk-ribbon roses, carnations, and daisies—in striking colors of flame red, ice blue, golden yellow, and flamingo pink—an almost three-dimensional effect is achieved. Finished with tiny yarrow flowers worked in French knots, and ivory seed beads, and sequins, this bag would be a perfect project for any seasoned embroider or an excellent challenge for a beginner.

Materials
16 x 20 in. (40 x 60cm) of dark navy linen for bag

16 x 20 in. (40 x 60cm) of heavyweight, woven interlining for bag

14 x 4¾ in. (35 x 12cm) of dark navy linen for handles

14 x 4¾ in. (35 x 12cm) of medium-weight, sew-in interfacing for handles

14 x 5½ in. (35 x 14cm) of dark navy linen for facing

14 x 5½ in. (35 x 14cm) of heavyweight, sew-in interfacing for facing

16 x 20 in. (40 x 50cm) of poppy red cotton lining fabric

⁵⁄₁₆-in. (7-mm) wide silk ribbon in flame red, ivory, ice blue, and pale olive green

Strong sewing thread in a neutral color

Pearl-shaped beads in ivory

⅛-in. (4-mm) wide silk ribbon in golden yellow, pale yellow, flamingo pink, and pale lilac

Pearlized seed beads in ivory

Metallic, cupped sequins in coral

Glass beads in pale pink

Fine chenille yarn in emerald green

Glossy rayon ribbon yarn in ivory and sunshine yellow

Embroidery floss in avocado and olive green

Sewing threads to match the navy linen and red lining fabrics

Magnetic clasp

Equipment
Template 2 (see page 136)

Fabric scissors

Long dressmaker's pins

White pencil

Large embroidery hoop

Small embroidery scissors

Embroidery needles in varying sizes

Fine sewing needle

Beading needle

Ruler

Iron

Sewing machine

Garden fresh

1 **Enlarge Template 2** by the amount stated and cut out the shape to make a paper pattern. Pin the pattern to the navy blue linen and draw around it, adding ¾ in. (2cm) for seam allowance and fabric shrinkage. Remove the pattern. Using the white pencil, lightly draw out the design, using the main photograph as a guide. Fit the fabric into the embroidery hoop (see page 16).

2 ▶ **To embroider the roses**, cut a length of the ⁵⁄₁₆ in. (7mm) ice blue silk ribbon. Thread one end into a needle and knot the other end. Bring the needle up through the center of a flower. Lay the ribbon flat then take the needle back down through the center of it and through the fabric, creating a small loop. Pull the needle and ribbon through; stop pulling as soon as the edges of the ribbon start to curl.

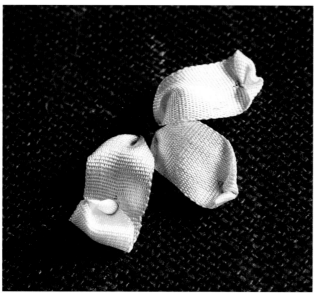

3 ▲ **Bring the ribbon** back up through the fabric at the center of the flower and repeat the same stitch until the five petals of a rose have been formed. Embroider all the blue roses in this way. Sew a pearl bead into the middle of each flower. Using a length of the ⅛ in. (4mm) golden yellow silk ribbon, sew the smaller rose flowers in the same way. Repeat with the pale yellow ribbon, too, until all the smaller flowers have been completed. Sew a seed bead into the center of each one.

4 ▲ **Using pale lilac silk ribbon**, embroider daisy flowers with the same technique, though this time give each flower more petals to form the daisy shape. Nine or ten petals should be sufficient. Work some of the daisies using flamingo pink ribbon. Sew a sequin topped by a pink glass bead into the center of each flower.

5 ▶ **Cut approximately** 8 in. (20cm) of the ⁵⁄₁₆ in. (7mm) flame red silk ribbon. Knot a single strand of sewing thread and starting at one end of the ribbon, work tiny running stitches along one edge.

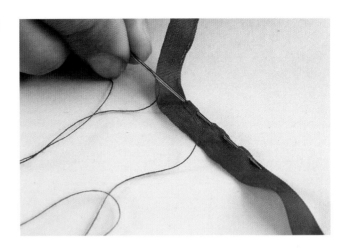

6 ▼ **Using an embroidery needle**, thread the end of the ribbon with the knot through the fabric, where you want the center of the flower to be. Begin to carefully gather the ribbon into a circle by pulling on the thread (see inset).

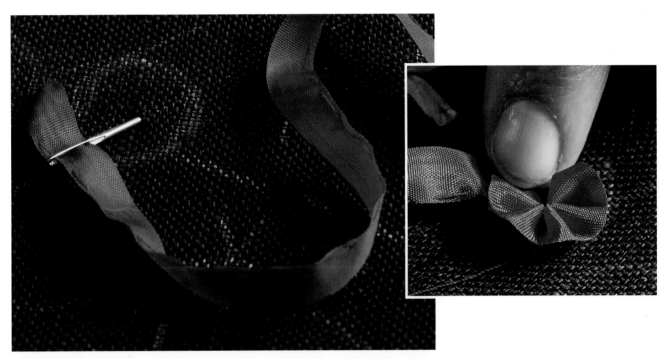

7 ◀ **Using another length** of thread, begin to sew the ribbon to the linen with tiny stitches along the gathered edge. Little by little, gather up more ribbon and curl it around, stitching the edge down as you go. Once the beautiful flower shape has been formed, cut off excess ribbon and carefully thread the end through the fabric and secure it with tiny stitches on the back. Repeat the process for the remaining flame red and ivory carnation flowers.

▶

Garden fresh

8 ▶ Using pale olive green ribbon, embroider a few leaves at the base of the stems, using the same technique as for the petals of the ice blue roses. Using the emerald green chenille yarn, sew a few scattered leaves in detached chain stitch, wherever you think they are needed.

9 ▲ Using the ivory rayon yarn, embroider some of the delicate yarrow flowers by making tiny French knots. Embroider the remaining yarrow using the pale yellow rayon.

10 ▲ Separating a few strands of olive green embroidery floss, embroider the slim stems in backstitch. Sew several smaller branches at the base of each yarrow, giving tiny stems to the French knotted flowers. Embroider the other stems using both olive green and avocado green floss.

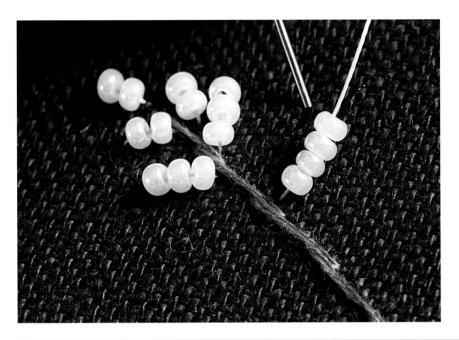

11 ◄ **Starting at the tip** of an empty stem, sew on a couple of ivory seed beads using the strong sewing thread. Work your way down the stem, sewing on the beads at a slight upward angle, increasing the number of beads on each branch of the sprig. When all the embroidery is complete, remove the fabric from the embroidery hoop and assemble the bag following the instructions for Medium Bag with Darts and Lined Handles (see pages 32–33), but substituting the folded handles from page 30. Tie a piece of yellow ribbon in a bow around one handle as a finishing touch.

Variation

This variation on the garden fresh bag is worked in pretty, feminine colors on a cream fabric to create a softer, vintage look. You can choose ribbon colors to accent a particular outfit, or just work in your favorite palette.

Summer chic

STITCHES USED
- **Fishbone stitch**
- **Satin stitch**

I found this gorgeous, rich, chocolate brown linen cloth in a local fabric store and fell in love with it immediately. I already had the variegated pink and green cotton yarns and thought they would be the perfect accompaniments. By embroidering large summer flowers in the yarns, using a raw silk fabric in a neutral color for the top band, and finishing it all off with antique brown sequins and gold ribbon, I created this simple yet stunning design.

Materials

16 x 20 in. (40 x 50cm) of chocolate brown linen fabric for bag

16 x 20 in. (40 x 50cm) of heavyweight, woven interlining for bag

14 x 9½ in. (35 x 24cm) of ecru raw silk fabric for contrast top

12 x 4¾ in. (30 x 12cm) of heavyweight, olive green linen for handles

12 x 4¾ in. (30 x 12cm) of medium-weight, sew-in interfacing for handles

14 x 4¾ in. (35 x 12cm) of ecru raw silk fabric for facing

14 x 4¾ in. (35 x 12cm) of heavyweight, sew-in interfacing for facing

16 x 20 in. (40 x 50cm) of peach-colored cotton lining fabric

Variegated cotton ribbon yarns in green/gold and pink

Strong sewing thread in a dark color

Large beads in gold

Small beads in antique gold

Cotton ribbon yarn in pink

Cupped sequins and small beads in antique brown

Sewing threads to match the brown linen, gold ribbon, olive green linen, ecru silk, and peach-colored lining fabric

Approx. 18 in. (45cm) of ribbon in gold

Magnetic clasp

Equipment

Template 2 (see page 136)

Fabric scissors

Long dressmaker's pins

White dressmaker's pencil

Embroidery hoop

Embroidery needles in varying sizes

Small embroidery scissors

Fine beading needle

Ruler

Iron

Sewing machine

Summer chic

1 ▶ **Enlarge Template 2** by the amount stated and cut out the shape to make a paper pattern. Pin the pattern to the brown linen fabric and draw around it, adding ¾ in. (2cm) for seam allowance and fabric shrinkage. Remove the pattern. Using the white pencil, lightly draw out the design, using the main photograph as a guide. Fit the fabric into the embroidery hoop (see page 16). Using a large-eyed needle and the variegated green yarn, embroider the leaves in fishbone stitch.

2 ▲ **Embroider the large flowers** in satin stitch, using the variegated pink yarn. Using the strong sewing thread, sew a large gold bead into the center of each flower.

3 ▲ **Using the strong sewing thread** again, sew on a ring of small gold beads around the large bead. Sew on two beads at a time.

4 ▶ Using the pink cotton yarn, embroider the small flowers in satin stitch, using three stitches to make each petal. Sew an antique brown bead into the center of each flower. Following step 7 of Sweet Lavender (see page 51), sew on sequins scattered within and around the embroidery, wherever you think they are needed.

Adding sequins

The number of sequins you sew on and where you put them is up to you. Just lay sequins on the design, move them until you are happy with the arrangement, then sew them on.

5 ◀ Remove the fabric from the embroidery hoop and sew the embroidered section to the contrast top band following steps 1–5 of Medium Bag with Darts and Lined Handles (see pages 32–33), but substituting the folded handles from page 30. Pin the gold ribbon to the brown linen, ¼ in. (5mm) below and parallel to the contrast top. Using the sewing machine and matching thread, sew down one edge of the ribbon. Starting at the same end, sew down the other edge. Finish assembling the bag according to the instructions.

Autumn bags

For my Autumn collection I have used rich, vibrant colors and cozy fabrics—such as warm wools and luscious velvets—to create bags that are aesthetically and emotionally in tune with the season. There's a range of styles to suit different needs or occasions. Choose a glamorous clutch bag for evening events, a roomy but stylish shoulder bag for when you really do need to carry a lot, or one of the two different styles of handheld bags that are perfect for daily use.

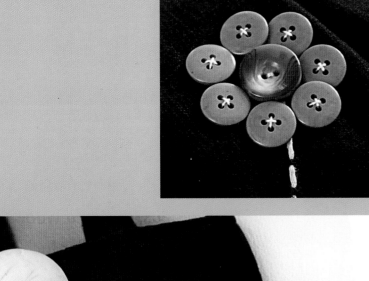

Lazy daisy

STITCHES USED
- **Daisy stitch**
- **Straight stitch**
- **Detached chain stitch**
- **Fishbone stitch**

This simple, uncomplicated bag uses chunky wool knitting yarns to create the oversized daisy flowers. Worked in contrasting, bright colors of magenta, lilac, and sable, on the sumptuous, deep red wool fabric, the design is highlighted with smaller fuchsia-colored flowers and finished off with bright, olive-toned leaves and lavender sprigs. A rich, chocolate brown velvet trim, button flower centers, and an extra-large central button detail complete the look.

Materials
16 x 20 in. (40 x 50cm) of rich red wool fabric for bag

16 x 20 in. (40 x 50cm) of heavyweight, woven interlining for bag

13½ x 16 in. (34 x 40cm) of chocolate brown velvet for top and facing

14 x 4¾ in. (35 x 12cm) of rich red wool fabric for handles

14 x 4¾ in. (35 x 12cm) of medium-weight, sew-in interfacing for handles

13½ x 16 in. (34 x 40cm) of heavyweight, sew-in interfacing for facing

16 x 20 in. (40 x 50cm) of chocolate brown satin lining

Chunky wool yarns in magenta, lilac, and sable

Twisted cotton yarn in fuchsia

Chenille yarn in lavender

Wool yarns in bright olive green and cream

Strong sewing thread in deep red

Three buttons in olive green

Sewing threads to match rich red wool fabric, chocolate brown velvet, and lining fabrics

Magnetic clasp

One oversized button in corn yellow

Equipment
Template 4 (see page 138)

Fabric scissors

Long dressmaker's pins

Pencil

Large embroidery hoop

Embroidery needles in varying sizes, including one with very large eye

Embroidery scissors

Fine sewing needle

Ruler

Iron

Sewing machine

Lazy daisy

1 ▼ **Enlarge Template 4** by the amount stated and cut out the main bag section to make a paper pattern. Pin the pattern to the textured, cream fabric and draw around it, adding ¾ in. (2cm) for seam allowance and fabric shrinkage. Remove the pattern. Using the pencil, lightly draw out the design, using the main photograph as a guide. Draw circles to indicate the outer edge of the daisies. Fit the fabric into the embroidery hoop (see page 16). Using the chunky lilac yarn and an embroidery needle with a large eye, begin by embroidering the largest flower in daisy stitch. Using the same stitch, embroider the other two flowers in the magenta and sable-colored chunky yarns.

Knitting yarns

The popularity of knitting has seen a huge increase in the types of yarns available. Many finer yarns are excellent for embroidery, but if you want to use thicker yarns you do need a forgiving fabric that lets the yarn pass through easily. Try the yarn you'd like to use on a swatch of fabric before starting a project.

2 ▲ **Using the fuchsia** cotton yarn, embroider the smaller flowers in a simple straight stitch. Start at the outer edge of the flower and work your way around the circle until you have filled it in. With the lavender chenille, embroider the tiny leaves on each of the sprigs in detached chain stitch. Start at the tip of each sprig and sew the leaves in matching pairs, running down the stem. To keep the design simple, you do not need to embroider a stem, as the leaves alone will give an indication of this.

3 ▶ **Using the bright** olive green yarn, sew the leaves using fishbone stitch. Keep the stitches tightly packed so that each leaf has a slightly raised appearance. To add detail, sew three straight stitches at the base of each leaf using the cream wool yarn. Make the central stitch long, with shorter stitches on either side.

4 ▼ **Sew a pale** olive green button into the center of each of the daisy flowers, using the strong, red sewing thread. If your buttons have four holes, like these, use a cross stitch to sew them on.

5 ▲ **Remove the fabric** from the embroidery hoop and assemble the bag following the instructions for Medium Bag with Pleated Top (see pages 34–35). To finish, sew the oversized corn-colored button to the top center of the bag front, again using the red sewing thread.

Vintage buds

Made in the deepest of sepia brown wool fabrics, this bag is trimmed with the same fabric in a soft sable color. With its tightly packed, ornately embroidered flowers and leaves in tones of cream, ivory, and beige—worked in a whole assortment of embroidery stitches and wool threads—this is a truly beautiful bag with a vintage twist.

STITCHES USED
- **Rose stitch**
- **Daisy stitch**
- **Detached chain stitch**

Materials
16 x 20 in. (40 x 50cm) of deep sepia brown wool fabric for bag

16 x 24 in. (40 x 60cm) of heavyweight, woven interlining for bag

14 x 5½ in. (35 x 14cm) of sable-colored wool fabric for contrast top band

14 x 4 in. (35 x 10cm) of deep sepia brown wool fabric for handles

14 x 4 in. (35 x 10cm) of medium-weight, sew-in interfacing for handles

14 x 4 in. (35 x 10cm) of antique gold satin lining fabric for handles

14 x 5½ in. (35 x 14cm) of deep sepia brown wool fabric for facing

14 x 5½ in. (35 x 14cm) of heavyweight, sew-in interfacing for facing

16 x 20 in. (40 x 50cm) of antique gold satin lining fabric

Selection of wool yarns in varying tones of cream, ivory, and beige

Strong sewing thread in brown

Beads and sequins in dark, rich, chocolate brown

Wool yarn in pale olive green

Sewing threads to match the sepia brown and sable-colored fabrics

Magnetic clasp

Equipment
Template 2 (see page 136)

Fabric scissors

Long dressmaker's pins

White pencil

Large embroidery hoop

Embroidery needles in varying sizes

Embroidery scissors

Beading needle

Iron

Ruler

Pinking shears

Sewing machine

Vintage buds

1 ▶ **Enlarge Template 2** by the amount stated and cut out the section below the horizontal dotted line to make a paper pattern. Pin the pattern to the sepia brown wool fabric and draw around it, adding ¾ in. (2cm) for seam allowance and fabric shrinkage. Remove the pattern. Using the white pencil, lightly draw out the design, using the main photograph as a guide. As this embroidery is so detailed, there is no need to draw out every single sprig as these can be simply added later where needed, in between the embroidered flowers. Fit the fabric into the embroidery hoop (see page 16). Begin by embroidering the rose-stitch flowers using doubled wool yarn in one of the shades of cream.

2 ▲ **Next, embroider the large daisies** in daisy stitch. Use all your cream, ivory, and beige yarns in turn to add subtle color variety to the embroidery.

3 ▼ **Using the palest cream yarn**, embroider the smallest flowers, which appear on the far left and right of the design, using detached chain stitch. Make sure you keep the stitches tightly packed, sewing five small petals for each flower. Sew a chocolate brown bead into the center of each flower using strong sewing thread.

4 ▼ **Using the strong** sewing thread again, sew a sequin into the center of each of the daisies. Sew on a few more sequins scattered over the bag as you wish.

5 ▲ **When all the flowers** have been worked, embroider the tiny sprigs in pale green yarn and detached chain stitch. Starting at the tip of each sprig, sew a single leaf followed by pairs of leaves. Vary the look, by giving some sprigs three leaves and some five. Fill in gaps in between flowers and around the outside edge of the band of embroidery.

6 ▶ **Remove the fabric** from the embroidery hoop and assemble the bag following the instructions for Medium Bag with Darts and Lined Handles (see pages 32–33). However, to add detail, replace steps 4–5 with the following process. Use pinking shears to carefully trim the top edge of the embroidered front and plain back main sections of the bag. Right sides up, lay the pinked edge on the lower edge of the sable-colored top section, overlapping them by ¾ in. (2cm). Using matching thread, topstitch the pieces together, stitching just below the pinked line. Sew the handles on to finish.

Fall blossoms

STITCHES USED
- **Buttonhole stitch**
- **Chain stitch**
- **Straight stitch**
- **Fishbone stitch**
- **Running stitch**

With its intense violet velvet trim and a single oversized coconut button, this gorgeous cream wool shoulder bag is both exquisite and practical. Buttonhole stitch is used to great effect to create large flowers in muted crimson merino wool. With large, detailed leaves in deep sepia and coffee brown and smaller sprigs in shades of burnt pumpkin, this subtly colorful bag is finished with large magenta beads and antique pink, gold, and brown beads and sequins.

Materials

22 x 24 in. (55 x 60cm) of heavyweight, cream wool fabric for bag

22 x 24 in. (55 x 60cm) of heavyweight, woven interlining for bag

14 x 6¼ in. (35 x 16cm) of heavyweight, violet velvet for contrast top band

4¾ x 26 in. (12 x 66cm) of wool fabric in camel for handles

4¾ x 26 in. (12 x 66cm) of medium-weight, sew-in interfacing for handles

14 x 6¼ in. (35 x 16cm) of heavyweight, violet velvet for facing

14 x 12¾ in. (35 x 32cm) of heavyweight, sew-in interfacing for facing

22 x 24 in. (55 x 60cm) of bright fuchsia satin lining fabric

Merino wool yarn in muted crimson

Fine wool yarn in deep sepia and coffee brown

Wool yarn in two shades of burnt pumpkin

Strong sewing thread in brown

Selection of sequins of varying sizes in antique acorn brown, pale pink and chocolate brown

Large round beads in metallic magenta

Small beads in antique gold

Sewing threads to match cream and camel-colored wools, violet velvet, and fuchsia pink lining fabric

Magnetic clasp

Oversized textured coconut button

Equipment

Template 6 (see page 140)

Fabric scissors

Long dressmaker's pins

Pencil

Large embroidery hoop

Embroidery needles in varying sizes

Small embroidery scissors

Beading needle

Ruler

Iron

Sewing machine

Fine sewing needle

Fall blossoms

2 ▲ **Using the fine wool yarn** in deep sepia, embroider the outline of some of the larger leaves in chain stitch. Embroider the central line of each leaf, too.

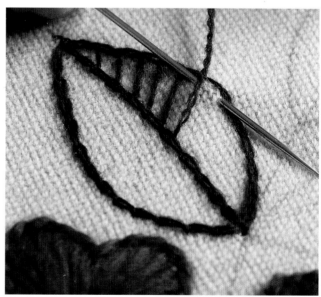

1 ▲ **Enlarge Template 6** by the amount stated and cut out the main bag section to make a paper pattern. Pin the pattern to the cream wool fabric and draw around it, adding ¾ in. (2cm) for seam allowance and fabric shrinkage. Remove the pattern. Using the pencil, lightly draw out the design, using the main photograph as a guide. Fit the fabric into the embroidery hoop (see page 16). Using the muted crimson yarn, embroider the large flowers in buttonhole stitch. Work your way around each flower, following the curved outline to form the petal shapes.

3 ▲ **To add detail** to these leaves, embroider simple, angled straight stitches on each side of the central chain-stitched line. Embroider the other large leaves in the same way, using the coffee brown fine yarn.

**4** ◄ **Using the lighter shade** of burnt pumpkin yarn and starting at the tip of one of the smaller sprigs, embroider the leaves in fishbone stitch. Work your way down the sprig, stitching the last two or three leaves at the base of the sprig in the darker shade of burnt pumpkin yarn. To add detail to these leaves, use the deep sepia yarn to sew a small straight stitch at the base of each leaf. In the same yarn, embroider the stems of these small sprigs with simple running stitch.

5 ► **Using the strong** sewing thread, sew on a selection of sequins scattered over the fabric, wherever you think they are needed.

6 ▲ **Sew a magenta bead** into the center of each of the flowers. In the same way as for step 7 of Les Roses (see page 71), sew a ring of antique gold beads around each magenta bead, attaching two beads at a time.

7 ▲ **Remove the fabric** from the embroidery hoop and assemble the bag following the instructions for Bag with Base and Top Pleats (see pages 38–39). To finish, sew the oversized coconut button to the center of the violet velvet on the front of the bag.

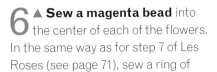

Verdant vine

STITCHES USED
- **Fishbone stitch**
- **Running stitch**
- **Straight stitch**

This glamorous clutch bag in the brightest fern green linen is simply stunning. The dazzling, daisy-style flowers are formed from diamond-cut, amber diamanté stones and conical wooded beads in cinnamon brown and grass green. They are detailed with golden beads and trailing leaves embroidered in rich saddle brown and intense sable. An edging of sparkling gold, flat sequins, and a tassel made of antique gold and amber beads with large, lime green wooden balls complete this sophisticated bag.

Materials
22 x 15¼ in. (55 x 38cm) of linen in bright fern green for bag

22 x 15¼ in. (55 x 38cm) of heavyweight, sew-in interfacing for bag

22 x 15¼ in. (55 x 38cm) of beige cotton lining fabric

15¼ x 8 in. (38 x 20cm) of heavyweight, sew-in interfacing for bag flap

Diamond-cut diamanté stones, one large oval and two smaller round ones in amber

Strong sewing thread in brown

Small beads in antique gold

Conical wooden beads in cinnamon brown and grass green, about twenty of each

Miniature gold sequins

Wool yarn in rich saddle brown and intense sable

Metallic gold rayon yarn

Small, cupped gold sequins

Flat gold sequins

Selection of amber and gold beads

Two large wooden ball beads in lime green

Sewing threads to match fern green linen and beige lining

Magnetic clasp

Equipment
Template 7 (see page 141)

Fabric scissors

Long dressmaker's pins

Pencil

Large embroidery hoop

Sewing needle

Small embroidery scissors

Embroidery needle

Beading needle

Ruler

Iron

Sewing machine

Verdant vine

1 ◀ **Enlarge Template 7** by the amount stated and cut out the shape to make a paper pattern. Pin the pattern to the fern green linen fabric and draw around it, adding ¾ in. (2cm) for seam allowance and fabric shrinkage. Arrange the amber stones on the bag flap where you would like the flowers to be, with the larger oval stone placed centrally on the flap and the two smaller stones at an equal distance on either side. Make sure you allow enough space for the wooden petals, gold beaded detail, and the sequined edging. Mark the position of the stones lightly with a pencil and draw out the trailing leaves. Fit the fabric into the embroidery hoop (see page 16). Using the strong sewing thread, sew on the amber stones at the marked points. Sew on a ring of antique gold beads around each stone, attaching two at a time.

2 ▲ **Using the strong** sewing thread, sew on the wooden beads in cinnamon brown and grass green around the edge of each stone, alternating the colors as you go.

3 ▲ **To add detail** to the flowers, sew a miniature gold sequin to the tip of each wooden "petal." Bring the needle up through the fabric at the edge of the sequin and take it back down through the central hole. Repeat on the other side of the sequin to attach it firmly.

4 ▲ **Using the saddle brown** yarn and fishbone stitch, and beginning at the central flower, embroider some of the leaves.

5 ◀ **With the same yarn**, sew the stems of the leaves with a simple running stitch. Use the metallic gold yarn to embroider three straight stitches at the base of each leaf. Embroider the remaining leaves in the intense sable yarn and detail them with gold yarn as well.

6 ▼ **To complete the design**, sew on the cupped gold sequins in and around the embroidery.

7 ◀ **Remove the fabric** from the embroidery hoop and assemble the bag following the instructions for Clutch Bag (see pages 40–41). To finish, sew a line of flat gold sequins around the flap, following step 7 of Sweet Lavender (see page 51). Start at one top corner and work your way around the curve, keeping the sequins close together.

8 ◀ **Lastly, create the** clasp detail by threading the glass amber beads, antique gold beads, and large lime green wooden balls onto strong sewing thread. Securely stitch them to the center of the flap edge to make two small beaded tassels.

Button flowers

This beautiful day bag is made in sumptuous, dark cinnamon brown linen fabric with muted kiwi green linen trim and textured ecru handles. The pale olive green and peacock blue buttons I have used to make the daisy flower shapes look striking against the brown linen. Finished with embroidered leaves and delicate sprigs formed using transparent buttons, this is an ideal project for a novice embroiderer.

STITCHES USED
- **Running stitch**
- **Fishbone stitch**
- **Straight stitch**
- **French knot**

Materials

16 x 20 in. (40 x 50cm) of dark cinnamon brown linen for bag

16 x 20 in. (40 x 50cm) of heavyweight, woven interlining for bag

13½ x 16 in. (34 x 40cm) of muted kiwi green linen for contrast top band and facing

14 x 4¾ in. (35 x 12cm) of textured ecru linen for handles

14 x 4¾ in. (35 x 12cm) of medium-weight, sew-in interfacing for handles

13½ x 16 in. (34 x 40cm) of heavyweight, sew-in interfacing for facing

16 x 20 in. (40 x 50cm) of cream cotton lining fabric

Cotton ribbon yarn in muted taupe

Wool yarn in coffee brown and rich chocolate

Twisted cotton embroidery floss in cream

Two buttons in peacock blue

Fourteen buttons in olive green

Twenty transparent buttons

Selection of sewing threads to match brown, green, ecru, and cream lining fabrics

Magnetic clasp

Large button in peacock blue

Equipment

Template 4 (see page 138)

Fabric scissors

Long dressmaker's pins

White pencil

Large embroidery hoop

Embroidery needles in varying sizes

Embroidery scissors

Ruler

Iron

Sewing machine

Sewing needle

Button flowers

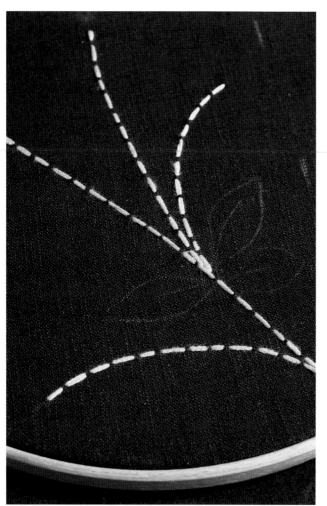

2 ▲ **Using the same yarn**, embroider the three large leaves in fishbone stitch. With the chocolate brown yarn, sew three straight stitches at the base of each leaf, making the central stitch slightly longer.

1 ▲ **Enlarge Template 4** by the amount stated and cut out the main bag section to make a paper pattern. Pin the pattern to the cinnamon brown linen and draw around it, adding ¾ in. (2cm) for seam allowance and fabric shrinkage. Remove the pattern. Using the white pencil, lightly draw out the design, making dots where the central button of each flower will go and using the main photograph as a guide. Fit the fabric into the embroidery hoop (see page 16). Using the taupe cotton yarn, sew the stems of the flowers and sprigs with running stitch.

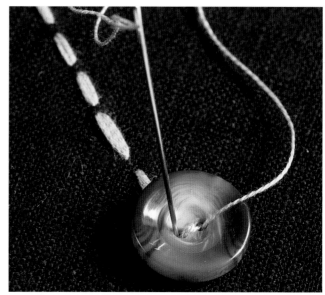

3 ▲ **Sew one of** the peacock blue buttons to the center of each daisy flower using the twisted floss.

4 ▲ **Lay seven olive green buttons** around one of
the blue button centers. Arrange them so they are
evenly spaced. Using the twisted cream embroidery floss,
sew on each button with a simple cross stitch. Repeat for
the second daisy flower.

5 ▲ **Starting at the tip** of each sprig, sew on a single
transparent button using the cream yarn. Sew on
buttons in pairs on either side of the sprig stem, leaving
a small space at the base to give a natural, botanical feel.
Add detail to the sprigs with a French knot in coffee
brown yarn on the outer edge of each button.

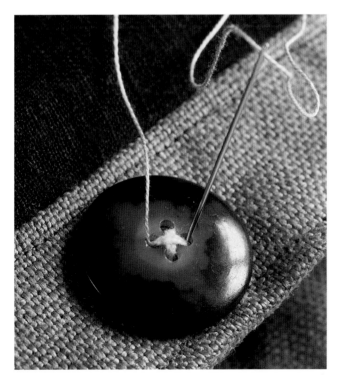

6 ◀ **Remove the fabric** from the embroidery hoop and
assemble the bag following the instructions for
Medium Bag with Pleated Top (see pages 34–35). To finish,
sew the large peacock blue button to the top center of the
bag front.

Winter bags

Bold color palettes and lots of metallic detailing are key notes in my collection of Winter bags. Whether they are created by lavish embroidery in gold, copper, and bronze, or the shimmer of stitched-on sequins, the metallic elements give a bag a fabulous, luxurious look. And you mustn't feel obliged to keep these bags for the evening only—they look great with day wear, too. Choose a bag with graphic color for a very different feel, but one that's just as versatile.

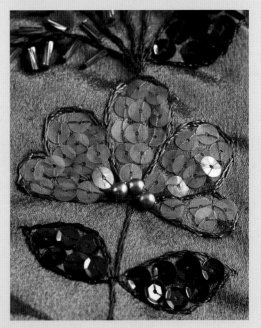

Fireside glow

STITCHES USED
- **Spider's web stitch**
- **Daisy stitch**
- **Satin stitch**
- **Running stitch**
- **Detached chain stitch**
- **Fishbone stitch**

This dazzling bag in fine, golden orange wool and sleek black satin is a truly opulent piece. A plethora of raised rose flowers in metallic silk organza and dupioni, and delicate flora in copper-colored rayon, metallic gold, and chocolate brown floss cover the bag front. Metallic beads, golden sequins, and a filigree button complete the very lavish look. The embroidery is worked on the satin, which is then appliquéd to the front of the bag during the assembly process.

Materials
16 x 8 in. (40 x 20cm) of black satin fabric for embroidery

16 x 24 in. (40 x 60cm) of fine wool fabric in golden orange for bag

16 x 24 in. (40 x 60cm) of heavyweight, woven interlining for bag

14 x 4¾ in. (35 x 12cm) of black velvet fabric for handles

14 x 4¾ in. (35 x 12cm) of medium-weight, sew-in interfacing for handles

14 x 5½ in. (35 x 14cm) of fine wool fabric in golden orange for facing

14 x 5½ in. (35 x 14cm) of heavyweight, sew-in interfacing for facing

16 x 20in. (40 x 50cm) of black satin lining fabric

Fine, twisted cotton embroidery floss in chocolate-brown

Metallic embroidery floss in both bright yellow-gold and aged antique gold

Glossy rayon embroidery floss in copper

24 x 4 in. (60 x 10cm) of metallic silk organza fabric in antique silver, cut into strips about 1¼ in. (3cm) wide

24 x 4 in. (60 x 10cm) of metallic dupioni silk fabric in old gold, cut into strips about 1¼ in. (3cm) wide

24 x 4 in. (60 x 10cm) of metallic viscose in bright gold, cut into strips about 1¼ in. (3cm) wide

Strong sewing thread in black

Selection of pearlized beads in chocolate brown and pale antique gold

Selection of sequins of differing sizes in tones of gold

7½ in. (70cm) length of gold sequins

Sewing threads to match the golden orange, chocolate brown lining, and black velvet fabrics

Magnetic clasp

Filigree antique gold button

Equipment
Template 2 (see page 136)

Fabric scissors

Long dressmaker's pins

White pencil

Large embroidery hoop

Embroidery needles in varying sizes

Embroidery scissors

Darning needle

Fine beading needle

Ruler

Iron

Sewing machine

Fireside glow

1 ▶ **Enlarge Template 2** by the amount stated and cut out the panel on the front to make a paper pattern. Pin the pattern to the black satin fabric and draw around it, adding ¾ in. (2cm) for seam allowance and fabric shrinkage. Remove the pattern. Using the white pencil, lightly draw out the design, using the main photograph as a guide. Indicate with circles the positions of the main roses and the daisy flowers. Don't worry too much about drawing every single sprig and leaf, as these can be just embroidered later in the spaces that remain. This will keep the design looking free and spontaneous. Fit the fabric into the embroidery hoop (see page 16). Using the chocolate-brown floss, sew the seven spokes of the spider's webs that will form basis of the rose flowers. Don't fill them in with fabric yet, as it's easier to complete the flatter embroidery before creating the three-dimensional roses.

2 ▲ **Embroider the daisies** in daisy stitch. Use the bright gold floss for some of them and the antique gold floss for the rest.

3 ▲ **Using the copper-colored** floss, embroider the tiny flowers in satin stitch, making each petal with four or five closely packed stitches.

4 ▲ **Using the chocolate brown** floss, embroider the sprig stems with running stitch. Starting at the tip of each stem, sew miniature leaves in detached chain stitch on each side. Add more of these sprigs wherever you think they are needed. Then embroider the larger leaves in fishbone stitch, sewing a small stem where needed with running stitch.

6 ▼ Using the strong sewing thread, sew a chocolate brown bead to the center of each of the daisies. Sew an antique gold bead to the center of each of the small, copper-colored flowers. Sew on gold sequins in any spaces that remain, and scattered around your design wherever you think they are needed.

5 ▲ Remove any loose threads from the edges of the strips of metallic fabric. Thread one end of a strip into the darning needle and fill in one of the spider's webs. Draw the fabric taut as you make each circle, going under and over the spokes so that they are well filled to create a beautiful, raised, rose shape. Repeat this step using the different metallic fabrics in turn until all of the roses have been filled in.

7 ◄ Cut out the panel. Press under the seam allowances on the top and bottom edges. Cut out a bag front in orange fabric and baste the panel to it, following the template. Lay a length of gold sequins along the top and bottom edges of the panel. Following step 5 of Wildflower Days (see page 79), machine sew the sequins in place, sewing the embroidered panel to the bag front at the same time.

8 ► Assemble the bag following the instructions for Medium Bag with Darts and Lined Handles (see pages 32–33), but substituting the folded handles from page 30. To finish, sew the decorative button to the top center of the bag front.

Black and cream

STITCHES USED
- **Running stitch**
- **Fishbone stitch**
- **Satin stitch**
- **Straight stitch**

This is an exceptionally sophisticated little bag that is the perfect accessory for any occasion, whether it be an evening cocktail party, a wedding breakfast, or a smart lunch. Made in natural fabrics—black linen and raw textured silk—it features a simple, elegant design worked in white and cream cotton yarns to give the classic styling a modern twist. The bag is finished with a mother-of-pearl disc and a black, diamond-cut button.

Materials

14 x 18 in. (35 x 45cm) of black linen fabric for bag

14 x 20 in. (35 x 50cm) of heavyweight, woven interlining for bag

12 x 12¾ in. (30 x 32cm) of ecru raw silk fabric for contrast top band and facing

14 x 4¾ in. (35 x 12cm) of ecru raw silk fabric for handles

14 x 4¾ in. (35 x 12cm) of medium-weight, sew-in interfacing for handles

12 x 6¼ in. (30 x 16cm) of heavyweight, sew-in interfacing for facing

14 x 16 in. (35 x 40cm) of cream cotton lining fabric

Thick, twisted cotton floss in white and beige

Strong sewing thread in black and cream

Small beads in black

Sewing threads to match the black linen, cream lining, and raw silk fabrics

Magnetic clasp

Mother-of-pearl disc with a hole smaller than the button

Black, diamond-cut, shank button

Equipment

Template 1 (see page 135)

Fabric scissors

Long dressmaker's pins

White pencil

Large embroidery hoop

Embroidery needles in varying sizes

Embroidery scissors

Fine beading needle

Ruler

Iron

Sewing machine

Black and cream

1 ▼ **Enlarge Template 1** by the amount stated and cut out the section below the horizontal dotted line to make a paper pattern. Pin the pattern to the black linen and draw around it, adding ¾ in. (2cm) for seam allowance and fabric shrinkage. Remove the pattern. Using the white pencil, lightly draw out the design, using the main photograph as a guide. Fit the fabric into the embroidery hoop (see page 16). Using the white floss, embroider all the stems in running stitch. Then use fishbone stitch to embroider the leaves.

Trims

The disc and button trim on this bag adds an interesting creative element. Keep an eye out for unusual trims and fastenings to use on your bags, including vintage brooches and buttons.

2 ▲ **Using the beige floss**, embroider the flowers in satin stitch. Start at the top of each stem, sewing single buds with three stitches. As you move down the stem, embroider budding flowers with three petals, each made with three stitches. Work a base for each bud consisting of four or five straight stitches in white floss.

3 ▶ **Embroider the fully open flowers** in satin stitch, working five petals of three stitches each for every flower. Using the black strong sewing thread, sew a bead into the center of each flower.

4 ▼ **Remove the fabric** from the embroidery hoop and assemble the bag following the instructions for Small Bag with Contrast Top, Darts, and Folded Handles (see pages 28–31). When the assembly is complete, lay the bag flat and position the mother-of-pearl disc on the top center front. Thread a needle with a length of cream strong sewing thread, knot the end and secure it in the center of the disc, where it will be hidden by the button.

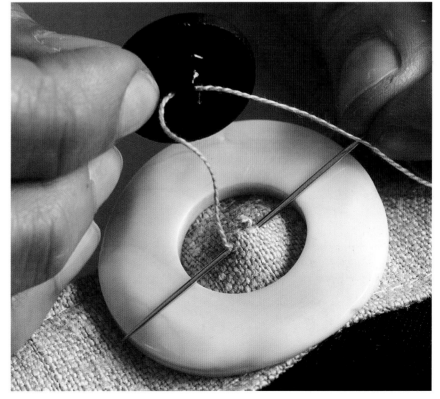

5 ▶ **Sew on the button** so that it is in the center of the disc. The disc can move, but it can't slip over the button.

Sparkling leaves

STITCHES USED
- **Chain stitch**

This shoulder bag uses a simple technique that both the novice and more experienced embroiderer can use to considerable effect. By choosing a patterned fabric you have a design to work from and build up with whichever embroidery stitches you choose. I loved the vintage look of this fabric and highlighted the graphic pattern with simple, outline chain-stitching and cup sequins. An oversized bow in plush, camel-colored wool fabric is a pretty finishing touch.

Materials
(Please follow the measurements below, but the precise color descriptions will depend on the patterned fabrics and contrasting trims you decide to choose.)

22 x 24 in. (55 x 60cm) of patterned fabric for bag

22 x 24 in. (55 x 60cm) of heavyweight, woven interlining for bag

14 x 6¼ in. (35 x 16cm) of camel-colored wool fabric for contrast top band

26 x 4¾ in. (66 x 12cm) of patterned fabric for handles

26 x 4¾ in. (66 x 12cm) of medium-weight, sew-in interfacing for handles

14 x 6¼ in. (35 x 16cm) of camel-colored wool fabric for facing

14 x 12¾ in. (35 x 32cm) of heavyweight, sew-in interfacing for facing

22 x 24 in. (55 x 60cm) of chocolate brown satin lining fabric

16 x 12 in. (40 x 30cm) of camel-colored wool fabric for bow

16 x 12 in. (40 x 30cm) of medium-weight, sew-in interfacing for bow

4 x 2½ in. (10 x 6cm) of camel-colored wool fabric for bow center

4 x 2½ in. (10 x 6cm) of medium-weight, sew-in interfacing for bow center

Rayon yarn in metallic gold

Strong sewing thread in a neutral color

Small, cupped, metallic sequins in antique gold, sepia, and slate blue

Glossy rayon embroidery floss in deep golden ochre

Sewing threads to match the patterned fabric, camel wool, and chocolate-brown lining

Magnetic clasp

Equipment
Template 6 (see page 140)

Fabric scissors

Long dressmaker's pins

Pencil

Large embroidery hoop

Embroidery needles in varying sizes

Small embroidery scissors

Fine sewing needle

Ruler

Iron

Sewing machine

Sparkling leaves

1 ▼ **Enlarge Template 6** by the amount stated and cut out the main bag section to make a paper pattern. Pin the pattern to the patterned fabric and draw around it, adding ¾ in. (2cm) for seam allowance and fabric shrinkage. Be aware of the placement of the pattern on the bag: I wanted the leaves to be in the middle and so I made sure they were central under the pattern piece. Remove the pattern and fit the fabric into the embroidery hoop (see page 16). Using the metallic gold rayon yarn, outline some of the leaves in chain stitch. Start at the base on one side and embroider right around the leaf.

2 ▲ **To add detail** to the leaves, sew a line of gold sequins up the middle, sewing them on as for step 7 of Sweet Lavender page (see page 51), and using the strong sewing thread. I have kept the sequins close together at the base and then gradually spaced them out as I worked up the central line. Embellish all the gold-outlined leaves in this way. Outline the remaining leaves in the golden ocher yarn and embellish them with sepia sequins.

3 ◄ **Other elements of** this pattern are highlighted with sewn-on lines of slate blue sequins.

4 ▶ **Remove the fabric** from the embroidery hoop and assemble the bag following the instructions for Bag with Base and Top Pleats (see pages 38–39). When the bag is complete, start assembling the bow. Lay the interfacing on the wrong side of the bow piece of fabric and, with right sides together, fold the piece of fabric in half lengthways, matching the raw edges. Pin the layers together.

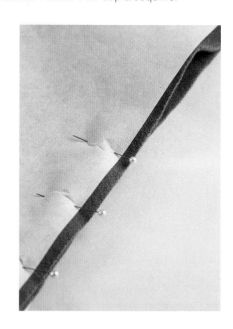

5 ▲ **Sew around the** open edges on the sewing machine, taking a ⅜ in. (1cm) seam allowance and leaving a small opening in one short side. Turn right-side out and press, pressing in the seam allowances across the gap.

6 ▲ **Topstitch all around** the rectangle in a matching thread, stitching ¼ in. (5mm) in from the edge and sewing right across the gap to close it.

7 ▲ **Lay the interfacing** on the wrong side of the bow center piece of fabric. Fold under ⅜ in. (1cm) along each long edge and pin. Topstitch all around the edges, as before.

8 ▲ **Pin one end** of the bow center to the middle of the back of the bow. Using your hands, pleat the fabric across the center to create the lovely bow shape.

9 ▲ **Wrap the bow center** right around the pleated bow. Join the ends at the back of the bow with several hand stitches.

10 ▲ **Using very small** hand stitches through the back of the bow center piece, carefully hand sew the bow to the center front of the bag.

Twinkling lights

STITCHES USED
- **Chain stitch**

Made from shimmering, turquoise satin fabric, this bag is a real work of art. Embellished with large daisy flowers chain stitched in slate blue rayon and filled in with pearlized flat sequins, the design also features trailing leaves filled with small cupped sequins in sapphire blue and deep navy, and dainty sprigs made out of the tiniest of seed beads in vivid iris blue and golden olive.

Materials

16 x 12 in. (40 x 30cm) of turquoise duchess satin for bag front

16 x 4 in. (40 x 10cm) of black, medium-weight cotton fabric for trim

16 x 12 in. (40 x 30cm) of black, medium-weight cotton fabric for bag back

16 x 24 in. (40 x 60cm) of heavyweight, woven interlining for bag

14 x 4¾ in. (35 x 12cm) of deep olive-green satin for handles

14 x 4¾ in. (35 x 12cm) of medium-weight, sew-in interfacing for handles

14 x 4¾ in. (35 x 12cm) of black, medium-weight cotton fabric for handle lining

14 x 5½ in. (35 x 14cm) of black, medium-weight cotton fabric for facing

14 x 5½ in. (35 x 14cm) of heavyweight, sew-in interfacing for facing

16 x 20 in. (40 x 50cm) of deep olive green satin lining fabric

Fine rayon floss in slate blue and muted slate blue

Strong sewing thread in blue and a neutral color

Pearlized translucent flat sequins

Cupped sequins in sapphire blue and deep navy

Emerald green sew-on diamanté stone

Round beads in antique gold

Bugle beads in bright turquoise

Seed beads in iris blue and also golden olive

Sewing threads to match turquoise, olive green lining, and black fabrics

29½ in. (75cm) length of gold, flat sequins

Magnetic clasp

Equipment

Template 3 (see page 137)

Fabric scissors

Long dressmaker's pins

Pencil

Large embroidery hoop

Medium-sized embroidery needle

Embroidery scissors

Beading needle

Ruler

Iron

Sewing machine

Twinkling lights

2 ▼ **Fill in each petal** with translucent sequins, sewing them on as for step 7 of Sweet Lavender (see page 51), using the strong sewing thread in neutral. Start at the base of a petal and work your way around the inner edge, finishing by filling in the space in the center. Make sure you place the sequins as close as possible to each other to cover the entire area of each petal.

1 ▲ **Enlarge Template 3** by the amount stated and cut out the shape to make a paper pattern. Pin the pattern to the turquoise satin and draw around it, adding ¾ in. (2cm) for seam allowance and fabric shrinkage. Remove the pattern. Using the pencil, lightly draw out the design, using the main photograph as a guide. Fit the fabric into the embroidery hoop (see page 16).Using the slate-blue floss, embroider the daisy flower shapes, outlining each petal with chain stitch. Embroider the main stems, smaller sprigs, and the outline of the large leaves in the chain stitch using the muted slate blue floss

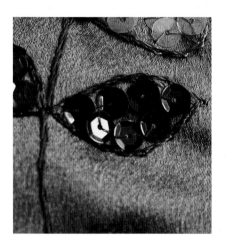

3 ◀ **Fill in the leaves** with sequins, using sapphire blue for some and deep navy for others.

4 ▶ **To finish the large flowers**, sew the single emerald diamanté stone into the center. Following step 7 of Les Roses (see page 71), sew on a ring of gold beads around the stone, but attach just one at a time.

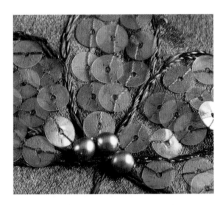

5 ▲ **Complete the remaining** flowers by sewing three gold beads to the base of each.

6 ▶ **Starting at the tip** of a main sprig and using strong thread, sew on bright turquoise bugle beads. Sew on each pair of beads at a slight angle, pointing upward, to give a more natural feel to each growing sprig. Work your way down the stem, leaving a small space at the base.

7 ◀ **Fill in the remaining sprigs** with seed beads, using golden olive beads for some and iris blue for others. Start at the top of the sprig by sewing on lines of three beads and as you work down the sprig, add more beads to each line.

8 **Remove the fabric** from the embroidery hoop. Cut the 16 x 4 in. (40 x 10cm) piece of black cotton fabric into two 16 x 2 in. (40 x 5cm) strips. With right sides facing, pin one of the strips to the base of the embroidery. Taking a ³⁄₈ in. (1cm) seam allowance, sew the pieces together. Press the seam toward the cotton fabric and topstitch. Fold the top of the embroidery as marked on the template. Pin the pleats in place, making sure the folds of fabric on the back face toward the center of the bag. With right sides facing, pin the remaining black cotton strip to the pleated top edge. Sew, press, and topstitch as before. Following step 5 of Wildflower Days (see page 79), sew a line of sequins to the seams at the top and bottom of the embroidery. Assemble the bag following the instructions for Medium Bag with Darts and Lined Handles (see pages 32–33).

Winter garden

This wool fabric bag combines textures, colors, and yarns to great effect, creating a truly dramatic accessory that will brighten up the dullest day. The vivid coral-colored cotton yarn, the pale lavender mohair, muted olive green chenille fibers, and fine twisted cottons in avocado and pistachio are mixed with large, pearl-drop beads in deep copper and soft, pale ivory to create this statement bag. Vivid magenta handles with contrast satin lining top off the design.

STITCHES USED
- **Satin stitch**
- **Straight stitch**
- **Detached chain stitch**
- **Running stitch**
- **Buttonhole stitch**
- **Daisy stitch**
- **Fishbone stitch**
- **Rose stitch**

Materials
16 x 24 in. (40 x 60cm) of heavyweight, black wool fabric for bag

16 x 24 in. (40 x 60cm) of heavyweight, woven interlining for bag

14 x 4¾ in. (35 x 12cm) of magenta wool fabric for handles

14 x 4¾ in. (35 x 12cm) of medium-weight, sew-in interfacing for handles

14 x 4¾ in. (35 x 12cm) of old-gold satin lining for handles

14 x 5½ in. (35 x 14cm) of heavyweight, black wool fabric for facing

14 x 5½ in. (35 x 14cm) of heavyweight, sew-in interfacing for facing

16 x 20 in. (40 x 50cm) of old-gold satin lining fabric

Cotton ribbon yarn in bright coral

Wool yarn in ivory and baby blue

Fine, twisted cotton yarn in avocado and pistachio

Strong sewing thread in black

Large drop-pearl beads in soft ivory

Pearl beads in deep copper

Thick mohair yarn in pale lavender

Chenille yarn in muted olive

Sewing threads to match black wool, gold lining, and magenta wool fabrics

Magnetic clasp

Equipment
Template 2 (see page 136)

Fabric scissors

Long dressmaker's pins

White pencil

Large embroidery hoop

Embroidery needles in varying sizes

Embroidery scissors

Beading needle

Ruler

Iron

Sewing machine

Winter garden

1 ▶ **Enlarge Template 2** by the amount stated and cut out the shape to make a paper pattern. Pin the pattern to the black wool fabric and draw around it, adding ¾ in. (2cm) for seam allowance and fabric shrinkage. Remove the pattern. Using the white pencil, lightly draw out the design, using the main photograph as a guide. Fit the fabric into the embroidery hoop (see page 16). Using the coral-colored yarn, embroider the large rose flowers in satin stitch. As these flowers are big, you will need to sew the outer edge of each petal first to form the shape, then fill in any space that remains with more satin stitch. To add detail to the flowers, use the ivory yarn to make three straight stitches at the base of each petal, making the central stitch slightly longer.

2 ▲ **Using the ivory yarn**, embroider the tiny budding sprigs in detached chain stitch. Start at the tip of each stem and work down, embroidering one petal for each small bud and three petals for budding flowers.

3 ▲ **Finish the sprigs** by embroidering stems in avocado cotton and running stitch. Add little leaves of detached chain stitch either side of each bud. Work four or five buttonhole stitches to make a base for each budding flower. Add more leaves where you think they are needed.

4 ◄ **Using the baby blue yarn**, embroider the smaller daisy flowers with daisy stitch. Embroider their leaves in fishbone stitch using the avocado cotton. Sew a pearl bead into the center of each daisy using the strong sewing thread.

5 ▼ **Sew a pearl bead** into the center of each rose. Following step 7 of Les Roses (see page 71), sew a ring of copper-colored beads around each pearl.

6 ◄ **Embroider the roses** using the lavender mohair yarn and rose stitch. Remember to use the yarn doubled to create shape and volume, keeping the stitches loose. Using the muted olive chenille yarn, embroider all the larger leaves in fishbone stitch. To add detail to these leaves, work straight stitches at the base of each in the ivory wool yarn, making the central stitch slightly longer. Remove the fabric from the embroidery hoop and assemble the bag following the instructions for Medium Bag with Darts and Lined Handles (see pages 32–33).

Beads

You can buy beads of all shapes and sizes in any good notions or crafts store. Look out for unusual beads that will add interest and a touch of individuality to your bag. Buy these beads when you see them and they'll be ready and waiting for the right bag.

Templates

On the following pages are the templates for the different styles of bag. The assembly instructions on pages 28–41 tell you which template you need for which bag. Each template gives the percentage to enlarge it by, plus there are measurements to help you

check that your paper patterns are the correct size.

The paired short lines on the top edge of each bag show the positions of the handles, while dashed and dotted lines show contrast top bands, facings, and darts, as appropriate to the style of the bag.

Projects using Template 1
- Bow and bouquet (see pages 52–57)
- Black and cream (see pages 118–121)

Projects using Templates 2 and 3
- Pink and pretty (see pages 58–61)
- Wildflower days (see pages 76–79)
- Garden fresh (see pages 80–85)
- Summer chic (see pages 86–89)
- Vintage buds (see pages 96–99)
- Fireside glow (see pages 114–117)

- Twinkling lights (see pages 126–129)
- Winter garden (see pages 130–133)

Projects using Template 4
- Lazy daisy (see pages 92–95)
- Button flowers (see pages 108–111)

Projects using Template 5
- First bloom (see pages 44–47)
- Forest blossoms (see pages 62–65)
- Les roses (see pages 68–71)

Projects using Template 6
- Red hot (see pages 72–75)
- Fall blossoms (see pages 100–103)
- Sparkling leaves (see pages 122–125)

Projects using Template 7
- Sweet lavender (see pages 48–51)
- Verdant vine (see pages 104–107)

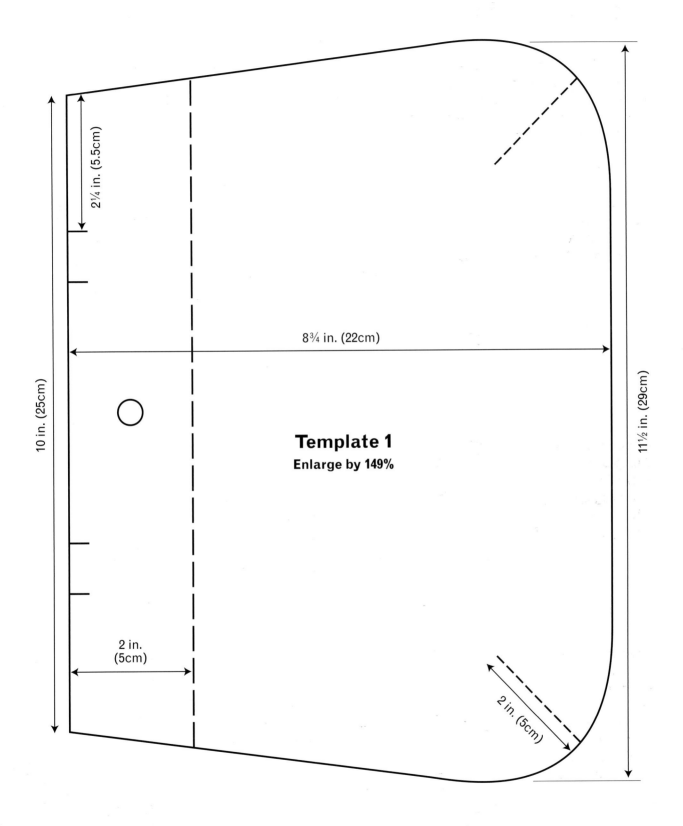

2¼ in. (5.5cm)

8¾ in. (22cm)

10 in. (25cm)

11½ in. (29cm)

Template 1
Enlarge by 149%

2 in.
(5cm)

2 in. (5cm)

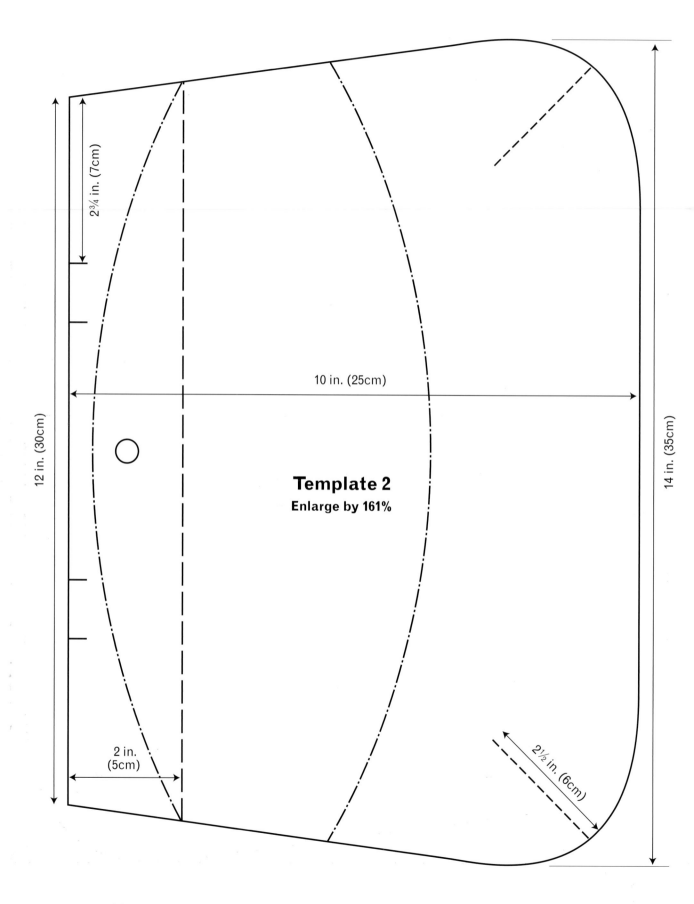

2¾ in. (7cm)

10 in. (25cm)

12 in. (30cm)

14 in. (35cm)

Template 2
Enlarge by 161%

2 in.
(5cm)

2½ in. (6cm)

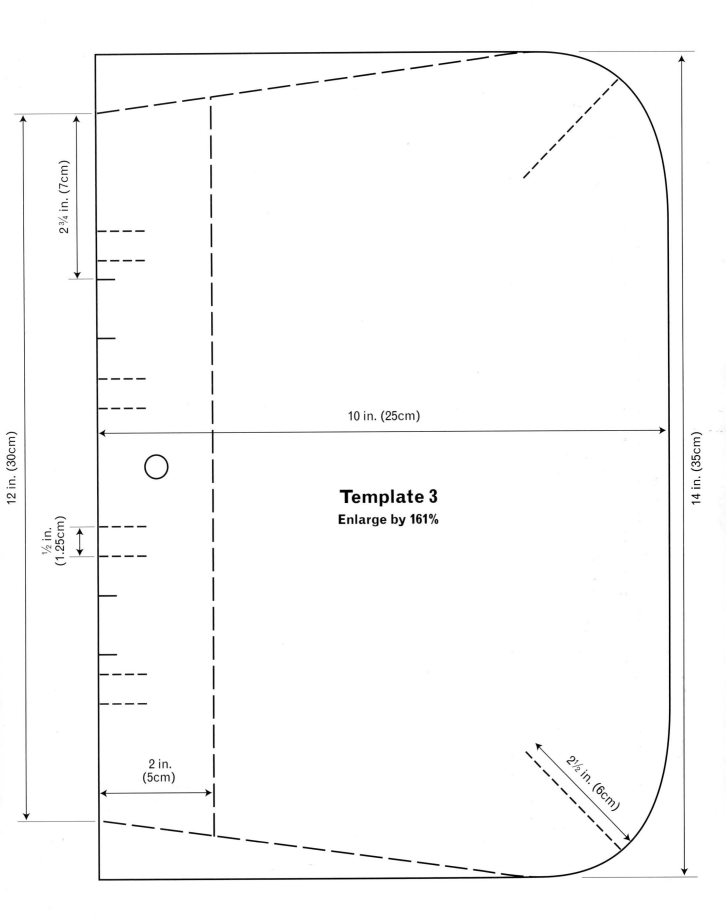

2 ¾ in. (7cm)

12 in. (30cm)

½ in. (1.25cm)

10 in. (25cm)

Template 3
Enlarge by 161%

14 in. (35cm)

2 in. (5cm)

2½ in. (6cm)

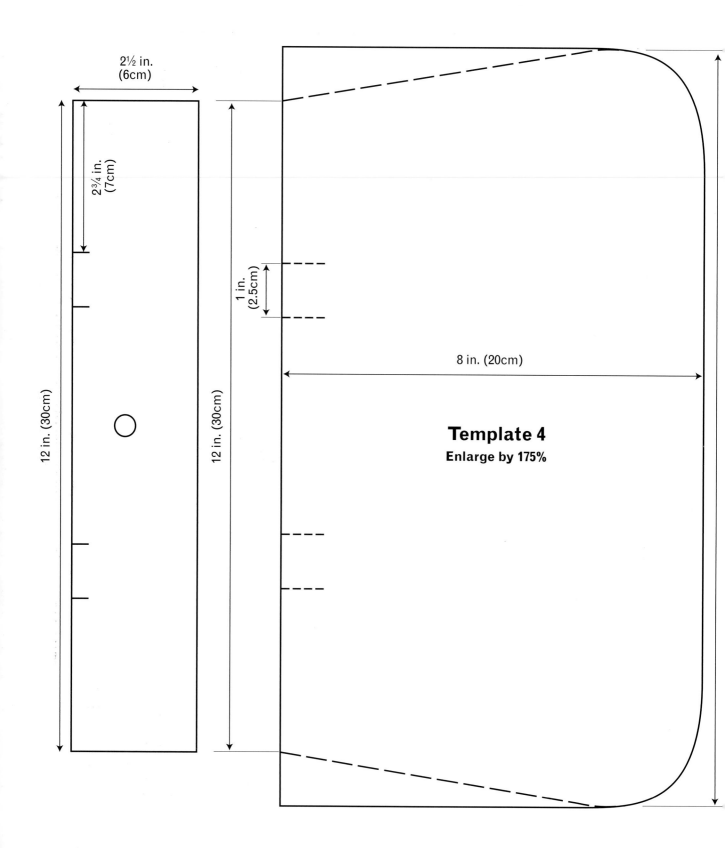

2½ in.
(6cm)

2¾ in.
(7cm)

1 in.
(2.5cm)

12 in. (30cm)

12 in. (30cm)

8 in. (20cm)

Template 4
Enlarge by 175%

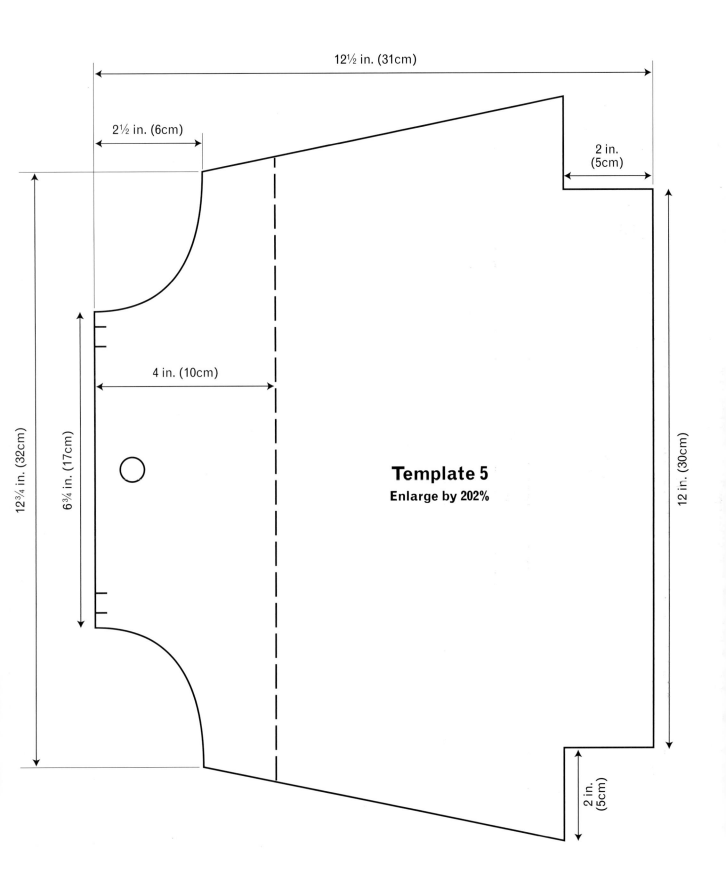

12½ in. (31cm)

2½ in. (6cm)

2 in. (5cm)

4 in. (10cm)

12¾ in. (32cm)

6¾ in. (17cm)

12 in. (30cm)

Template 5
Enlarge by 202%

2 in. (5cm)

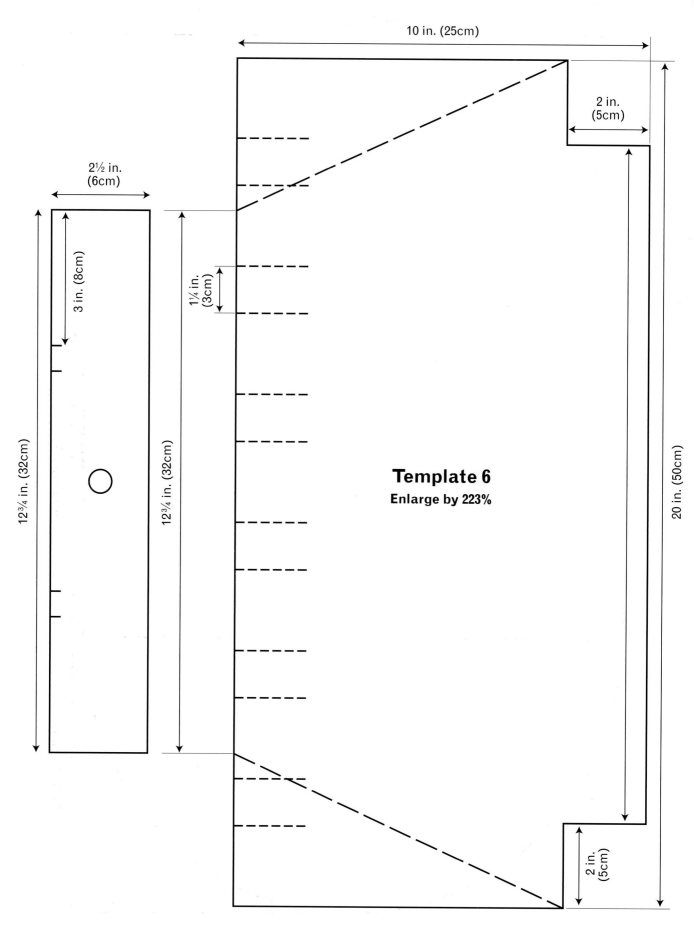

10 in. (25cm)

2½ in. (6cm)

2 in. (5cm)

3 in. (8cm)

1¼ in. (3cm)

12¾ in. (32cm)

12¾ in. (32cm)

20 in. (50cm)

2 in. (5cm)

Template 6
Enlarge by 223%

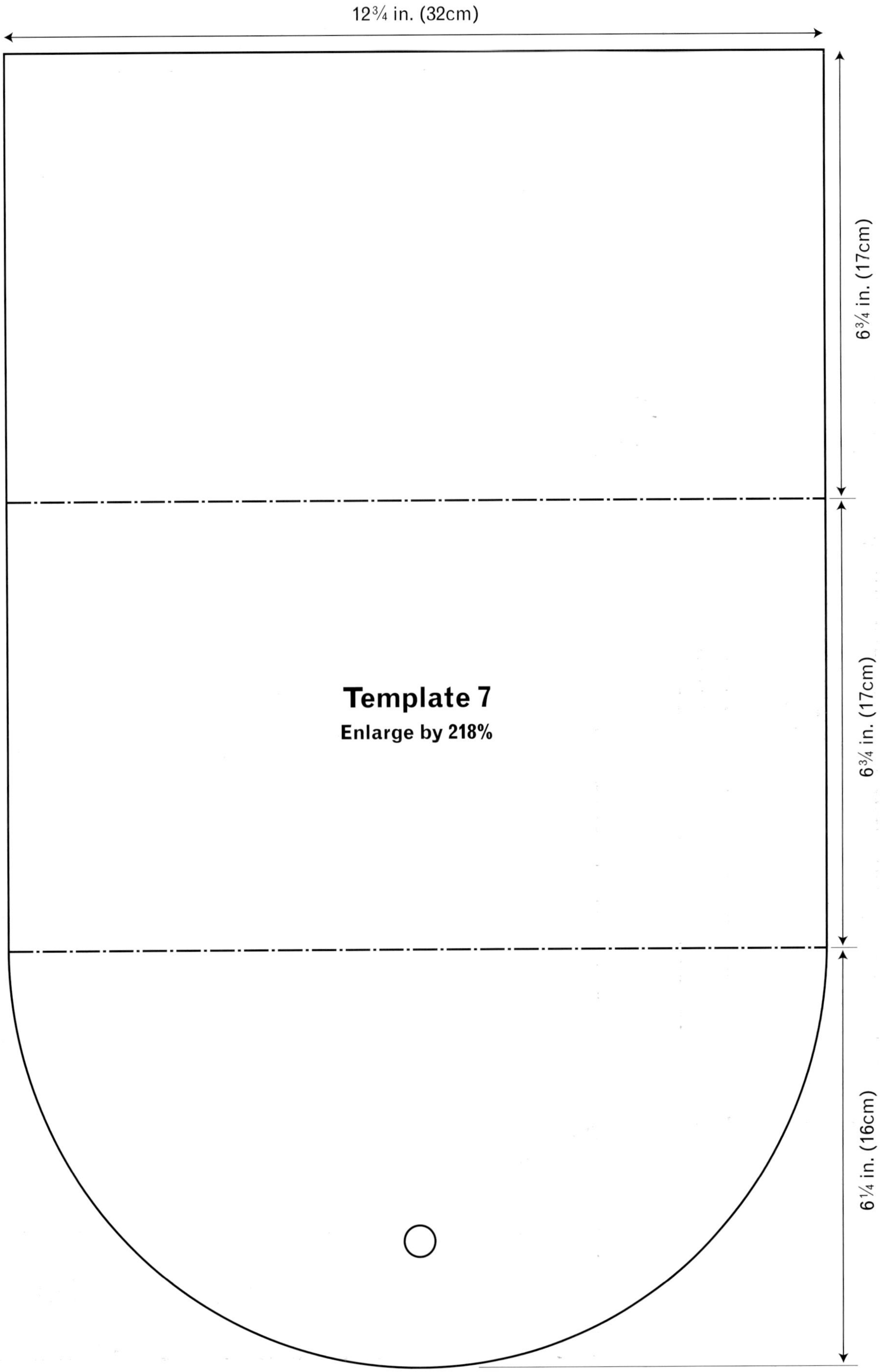

12¾ in. (32cm)

6¾ in. (17cm)

Template 7
Enlarge by 218%

6¾ in. (17cm)

6¼ in. (16cm)

Resources

A.C. Moore
www.acmoore.com
1-888-ACMOORE (1-800-226-6673)

Anchor
www.coatsandclark.com
1-800-648-1479
To purchase online:
www.theyarncollection.com
1-877-292-0062
CustomerService—CC@herrschners.com

DMC
www.dmc-usa.com
973-589-0606
dmcusa@dmcus.com

Hobby Lobby
www.hobbylobby.com
For mail order or online purchasing:
www.craftsetc.com
1-800-888-0321

Jo-Ann
www.joann.com
1-888-739-4120

Kreinik
www.kreinik.com
1-800-537-2166
info@kreinik.com

Michaels
www.michaels.com
1-800-MICHAELS (1-800-642-4235)

Weeks Dye Works
www.weeksdyeworks.com
877-OVERDYE (1-800-689-7393)
contact@weeksdyeworks.com

YLI
www.ylicorp.com
1-803-985-3100
www.ylicorp.com

About the author
Susan Cariello has been a textile print designer for
over fifteen years, working in New York and London.
Specializing in embroidery techniques and
embellishment, she creates her collections of unique
hand-made bags and accessories in her studio in
Norwich, England. Susan can be contacted through
her website at www.susancariello.co.uk for
information on commissions, stockists, and to keep
up to date with shows and exhibitions.

Index

Acknowledgments

A big thank you to Jane Birch for spotting me and my bags at The Country Living Fair, London.

A big thank you to Kate Haxell for working with me on this my first book, and for all her support, advice and encouragement.

A big thank you to Sussie Bell for her fantastic photographs of all my embroidered bags.

A big thank you to Kate Simunek for the beautiful illustrations and to Lisa Tai for the lovely page design.

Also, a big thank you to Janet Ravenscroft and everyone at Breslich & Foss for all their help, advice, and enthusiasm for both me and my bags, without which none of this would have been possible!